THE MAIL MUST GO THROUGH

THE STORY OF
THE PONY
EXPRESS

THE MAIL MUST GO THROUGH

THE STORY OF
THE PONY
EXPRESS

Margaret Rau

MORGAN
REYNOLDS
PUBLISHING
Greensboro, North Carolina

THE AMERICAN WEST

The Pony Express
Sam Houston
Belle Starr
Ishi
Mary Draper Ingles
Olive Oatman

Library of Congress Cataloging-in-Publication Data

Rau, Margaret.
    The mail must go through : the story of the Pony Express / Margaret
        Rau.— 1st ed. p. cm.
Includes bibliographical references and index.
    ISBN-10: 1-931798-63-X (library binding)
    ISBN-13: 978-1-931798-63-1 (library binding)
    1. Pony express—Juvenile literature. I. Title.
    HE6375.P65A38 2005
    383'.143'0973—dc22
                                        2005003061

My thanks to Larry Carpenter, corresponding secretary of the National Pony Express Association, for providing me a wealth of valuable information.

Contents

A Pony Express rider passes workers constructing the telegraph system that will eventually contribute to the demise of the legendary mail delivery system. *(Courtesy of the Granger Collection.)*

CHAPTER ONE

From the East

In January of 1860, William Russell and his son John sent out a press release to newspapers across America. Its contents immediately appeared in headlines across the nation. The Leavenworth *Daily Times* ran a screaming banner: "GREAT EXPRESS ADVENTURE! FROM LEAVENWORTH TO SACRAMENTO IN TEN DAYS! CLEAR THE TRACK AND LET THE PONY COME THROUGH!"

The story went on to explain that the new Central Overland California & Pike's Peak Express Company, formed by the well-known transportation moguls Russell, Majors & Waddell, was launching a Pony Express in April. Its purpose was to offer mail service between the East and West coasts.

Many people who saw the newspaper stories

Mail-delivery entrepreneur John Butterfield.

laughed at the idea of accomplishing such a feat. The problem was distance—how could almost 2,000 miles, most of it rugged wilderness broken by towering mountain ranges and waterless deserts, be crossed in ten days no matter what the weather?

At the time the Pony Express was founded, most cross-country mail was carried on the stagecoaches provided by the Butterfield Overland Mail Company, founded by John Butterfield. The Butterfield route started in Independence, Missouri, and went south on the Oxbow trail, avoiding most of the mountains in the region by dipping into El Paso, Texas, and then continuing on to Fort Yuma in southern Arizona. From there a branch ran north to Sacramento, avoiding the Sierra Nevada, which were impassable for stagecoaches and often even for mule-drawn wagons when winter swept in blizzards and heavy snows.

The Butterfield route was relatively easy but it was also long; it often took stagecoaches three weeks to get

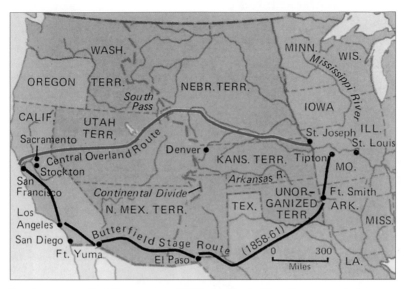

The Central Overland Route, proposed for use by the Pony Express, was far more direct, but also more risky, than the Butterfield Stage Route.

from Independence to Fort Yuma. Then it would take another week or so for the mail to travel north to Sacramento, California's capital. In 1860, there was no transcontinental telegraph or railroad. Much of the land between Missouri and California was unorganized and sparsely populated territory. California had gained statehood in 1850 during the gold rush years, but Utah, New Mexico, Arizona, Colorado, Nebraska, the Dakotas, Nevada, Montana, Washington, Idaho, Wyoming, and Oklahoma had not yet entered the Union. The lonely miners, farmers, and business people out in California were excited about the prospect of getting their mail in a more timely fashion. Mail sent on ships traveled from one coast to another by way of the Isthmus of Panama. Since no canal had yet been built, one ship's cargo was

Butterfield Overland stagecoaches carried passengers as well as mail through the largely unsettled West during the mid-1800s. *(Wells Fargo Bank History Room)*

loaded onto a railroad to be hauled across that narrow strip of land and packed onto another ship on the other side.

Russell and his partners were planning to bring mail across what was called the central route—a more dangerous but quicker trip across the Sierra Nevada and into Sacramento. The Chorpenning firm already used the central route, but their drivers took slow mule trains and were often defeated by the winter weather. Russell and his firm bought the Chorpenning contract, planning to augment the slow mule-train service with a Pony Express. It would not only be faster but would also deliver at all times of the year, winter as well as summer.

William H. Russell was the mastermind behind the

Pony Express founder William H. Russell.

idea for the Pony Express. His forte was ideas—not the
practicalities of implementing them. William B. Waddell,

William Waddell.   Alexander Majors.

an economist, made it his job to keep close watch over expenditures. He realized that the venture would be an expensive and risky undertaking because Russell had not yet been able to get the government to grant them a subsidy for mail delivery on this route. Everything would have to be financed with private funds until, as Russell hoped, the government recognized the value of the service and came through with the subsidy.

The third member of the firm, Alexander Majors, had grown up in the transportation service and was an expert freighter. A devout Christian, Majors was also concerned with preserving the morality of the men who worked for him. With temptations of all kinds rampant on the western frontier, he required his employees to sign a pledge that read: "While I am in the employ of A. Majors I agree not to use profane language, not to get drunk, not to gamble, nor to treat the animals cruelly, and not to do anything incompatible with the conduct of a gentleman. I agree if I violate any of the above conditions to accept my discharge without any pay for my services." Each employee was given a Bible.

The plan for the Pony Express that Russell, Majors & Waddell had put together looked quite simple on paper. It wasn't a novel concept, either. Pony expresses had been used before as a means of moving information to and through rural areas. What was impressive about this plan was its scope—the sheer amount of territory it planned to cover. It was understood that a single rider could not cover some 2,000 miles in ten days. But relays of riders and horses could. The relays of riders would start at two terminal stations—one in Sacramento, California, and the other in St. Joseph, Missouri. A well-established train service east of the Mississippi would bring the mail to the frontier town of St. Joseph.

From St. Joseph in the East and from Sacramento in the West, the mail would be passed from rider to rider until the last rider from the West met the last rider from the East. At this midway point the riders would exchange pouches and return the way they had come.

On the eastern section of the route the Pony Express would be able to use a number of stations that had been built to service the stagecoaches already running. These

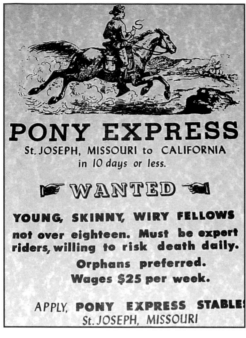

PONY EXPRESS

St. JOSEPH, MISSOURI to CALIFORNIA
in 10 days or less.

☞ **WANTED** ☜

YOUNG, SKINNY, WIRY FELLOWS
not over eighteen. Must be expert
riders, willing to risk death daily.
Orphans preferred.
Wages $25 per week.

APPLY, **PONY EXPRESS STABLE**
St. JOSEPH, MISSOURI

An advertisement recruiting riders.

stations were located eighty-five to one hundred miles apart. A good rider could go a hundred miles or more at a stretch, but a horse running at breakneck speed could not last much more than fifteen miles without collapsing. This meant that many more relay stations would be needed. Many people were convinced they could not be built in the three months allotted before the service began. Russell, Majors & Waddell ignored all the doubters and sent teams of surveyors to mark fifteen-mile lengths along the route.

Workers followed close behind the surveyors to begin putting up the stations needed. Where there were trees they built wooden houses. On the treeless prairies they made sod stations out of blocks cut from the root-bound prairie soil. In the desert they made sun-dried adobe bricks and built small huts. In several places they dug out cave homes in the sides of rough canyon walls. In most of the stations the men's quarters were primitive, but the horses were always given the best of everything because so much depended on them.

There had to be a lot of horses. The firm chose only the best. Some came from Kentucky's high-grade stock. Farther west they sought out half-breed mustangs famous for their speed and endurance. The firm bought five hundred horses in all.

To everyone's amazement, things were almost ready for the first run by March. Just two more important decisions had to be made. The firm would have to select the men who were to manage the individual stations and the riders who would carry the mail. Already, ads for these riders had been placed in newspapers in the East and the West. Interested applicants were told to apply at the Patee House, the firm's headquarters in St. Joseph, or at the firm's headquarters in Sacramento. Soon the dusty streets of St. Joseph and Sacramento began to swarm with prospective riders.

Some were wild mountain men in buckskins. In the West, young miners tired of trying for riches in newly opened gold and silver fields threw away their shovels for a horse. Ranch workers looking for more excitement joined the throngs of applicants. From the prairies came farm boys in faded red shirts and denim pants. They had grown weary of the endless routines of plowing and sowing and reaping. There were even a few Easterners lured from the Atlantic seaboard by the promise of wilderness adventures.

Though these young people came from different walks of life, they had two things in common: they knew how to ride and handle a horse, and they all craved excitement, even if it meant danger.

By this time, people had stopped joking about the idea of the Pony Express. Instead, newspapers in the East and in the West were heralding the extraordinary feat performed by the spunky firm of Russell, Majors & Waddell. Instead of giving up on what seemed an impossible dream, they had persevered. Now they were going to keep to their promise to start the great relay race on April 3.

In St. Joseph, people were milling around the Patee House where applicants were being interviewed for the privilege of working for the Pony Express. Older men with strong management skills were picked to staff the relay stations. Stock handlers and trainers were chosen for their knowledge of horses to keep them in good physical condition for the grueling relays. Relay riders were carefully screened and evaluated, and a cheer went up from the crowds when it was announced that eighty young men had been selected to run the first laps of the great race.

Heavier men were rejected no matter how skillful they were as horsemen. Their weight would slow down the horse. But even being skinny was not enough. The chosen men also had to be capable of riding more than a hundred miles at a time if necessary, even when that meant going day and night without sleep. And they had to be agile enough to transfer the mail pouches from a

The Patee House in St. Joseph, Missouri. *(Patee House Museum, St. Joseph)*

spent horse to a fresh one in minutes. Most of all, the riders had to be able to make quick decisions if threatened by danger from people, animals, or natural forces.

Most of the riders chosen were still in their teens. The few older ones were all single—the firm did not want riders with wives and children. Their focus had to be on the Pony Express's slogan: whatever the circumstances, the mail must go through.

For their services, the riders would be given room and board and a monthly salary ranging from fifty to one hundred dollars, depending on the difficulty of the lap to which they were assigned. That was a fair sum of money at a time when a good horse might cost about fifteen dollars, a shirt about a dollar, pants nearly ten, and a rifle around twenty-five. A pound of sugar was just a nickel. But most of the riders were not especially interested in the pay. They were there for the adventure and the glory.

The chosen men were boarded in the elegant Patee House. In town, they were treated like celebrities. They had only to swagger down the street to be greeted with cheers. They were guests at the fashionable dances that were held in the ballroom of the Patee House. These were strictly formal affairs. Women wore their party gowns— full skirts brushing the floor, hair piled high in the fashion of the day. Men wore black suits, waistcoats, and cravats. Their hair was neatly groomed, their mustaches newly trimmed.

This strict dress code was lifted for the riders. Many of them wore their lank hair long after the style of the frontiersmen. In their red shirts and blue jeans, or their buckskins and boots, they stood out in the midst of the elegance that surrounded them. The jingle of their spurs sounded in the pauses between the musical numbers of the band. Though their clothes were not proper ballroom attire and their manners were not elegant, the young men never wanted for partners. Women clustered around them, vying with one another for the honor of a dance.

Soon enough, the parties were over and the new managers, along with the riders, headed out to take up their posts at the new stations. Only one rider was left in St. Joseph. He would be the one to carry the mail on the first leg of the first Pony Express run.

Though many artists have taken the Pony Express as their subject and many writers have made the service famous, some uncertainties remain. Over the years, as the Pony Express made its way into the annals of American history, facts became less certain and stories grew more fantastic. What we have today is some combination

Four Pony Express riders. The man at the top left is thought to be Billy Richardson. *(St. Joseph Museum)*

of legend and truth, a testimony to the fascination inspired by this short-lived but dramatic enterprise.

Many reporters and witnesses were gathered in St. Joseph the day of the first run, but accounts of the momentous event differ. It is believed that the first rider was William (Billy) Richardson. An old photograph shows a slender young man with dark shoulder-length hair and a drooping mustache. He came from Virginia, and like many Virginians he was an expert horseman. For several years he had been a sailor, which meant he was well acquainted with hardship and danger.

As the first run of the Pony Express neared, merchants decorated the whole business center of St. Joseph. Flags fluttered from downtown buildings. Red, white, and blue bunting draped the storefronts. Cannons were placed before the entrance to the Patee House where the horse and rider would begin their dash. Council members invited the mayor to give a farewell speech, after which Richardson would mount his horse. The cannon would boom, and at exactly 5:00 PM he would gallop off.

All that was missing was the mail. It was coming from the East by train. The stationmaster had promised that it would arrive in time for the five o'clock send-off. As the day wore on, the crowds grew thicker and thicker along the street down which the pony would race. As five o'clock neared, the buzz became a roar. A trainer appeared, leading a bright bay-colored mare. He was going to give her a warm-up before the run, but suddenly a surge of people blocked his way. They were after souvenirs, hoping to get a few hairs from the horse's tail. The hairs could be woven into rings or watch chains, keepsakes of this historic day.

The mare whinnied, kicking and rearing as hands groped for her tail. The trainer had to struggle to keep the shuddering horse from bolting into the crowd. Pulling her along, he began pushing his way back through the thicket of grasping hands. If the horse became too spooked she couldn't make the run at all. Finally, the trainer got her to her stall in the stables. There she would stay, safely hidden away until five o'clock came and the train whistle sounded announcing the arrival of the mail. Then the ceremonies could begin.

The mail had first been collected in Washington, D.C., the nation's capital, and put in a special pouch. A messenger carrying the pouch then boarded a train for New York. When the train arrived on March 31, another pouch filled with letters and the latest newspaper editions was added. After a change of trains, the mail pouches were on their way to Detroit, Michigan.

Unfortunately, there were delays along the way, and the train arrived too late for the messenger to catch the early train for St. Joseph. The rail superintendent of Hannibal, Missouri, took charge. He ordered that the tracks to St. Joseph be kept clear and told the refueling stops along the way to have plenty of wood and able-bodied men on their platforms, ready to refuel the train when needed. Trains in that day ran on steam, so they always had to have a ready supply of wood or coal handy.

The train chosen to bring the mail to St. Joseph, the *Missouri,* was a little train: just one engine and one car. When the train from New York finally arrived, two-and-a-half-hours late, the pouch and its keeper were quickly loaded aboard the *Missouri,* which then headed down the tracks at twenty miles an hour. The speed rose to thirty, then to forty. Swaying dangerously from side to

The steam engine *Missouri,* which carried the Pony Express's first run of mail to St. Joseph. *(St. Joseph Museum)*

side, the train rushed on. Fields, trees, and houses sailed by. At platform after platform the train stopped to refuel. Men waiting with loads of wood dropped them into the tender, and with scarcely a pause, the train rushed on, eating up the miles.

In St. Joseph, men with megaphones announced the message telegraphed from the Hannibal superintendent. The mail was on its way—but the train would be at least two-and-a-half-hours late. At this news there were mutterings on all sides, but few people left. To provide the restless crowds with some kind of entertainment, the brass band played number after number until finally a whistle announced the arrival of the little *Missouri.*

The *Missouri* had made its run of more than two hundred miles in less than five hours, establishing a record that would stand for half a century. The messenger carrying the mail alighted from the passenger car and hurried to the Patee House with the pouches. Every letter in them had been written on tissue-thin paper because the amount of mail the Pony Express riders could carry was limited to twenty pounds. Any more would slow down the horse.

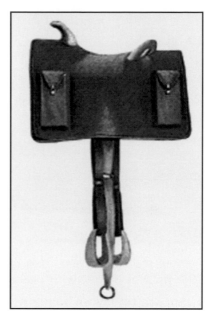

A mochila typical of those used by Pony Express riders.

At the Patee House, the letters and papers were wrapped in oiled silk to protect them from rain along the way. While this was being done, the mare was brought out and saddled. Then an attendant arrived with the mochila. Mochila is a Spanish word meaning "leather made." The mochila was a large piece of leather, with a leather box dangling from each of its four corners.

The attendant threw the mochila over the pony's saddle. A slit at the front of the mochila slipped over the saddle horn. Another slit at the back of the mochila fit over the cantle. This firmly anchored the mochila in place. The bundled-up letters and papers were placed in three of the leather boxes attached to the mochila. The boxes were then locked. The only people to hold keys to them would be the station managers at St. Joseph and Sacramento. The fourth box was left open to collect mail along the way.

The town of St. Joseph, Missouri, in 1861, as seen from the Kansas side of the Missouri River. *(University of California)*

Even though the Pony Express was getting a late start, the planned ceremony could not be canceled. After all, 1860 was an election year. The first speaker was Mayor M. Jeff Thompson, who was running for reelection. He delivered a long address aimed chiefly at voters.

The mayor was followed by Alexander Majors, who spoke about the history his firm's latest endeavor was about to make. An experienced frontiersman himself, Majors knew well the dangers his riders might face. But he had faith in their ability.

After the speeches ended, the cannon was fired and the first rider of the Pony Express galloped down the main street of St. Joseph, headed due west.

The initial run was short—just down to the Missouri River where a ferry was waiting to carry horse and rider across the brown waters to the western shore. On the ferry the rider probably shed the awkward rifle he was carrying. Eventually, all the riders would discard theirs, along with one of the two pistols they were issued—speed was of the utmost concern.

Beyond the river, the road ran straight and true through the countryside. By 11:30 PM, Billy Richardson finished his last lap at Seneca. He had cut the lost time down by forty-five minutes.

Dan Rising and his horse were waiting to take Richardson's place. The mochila was transferred and the second man in the relay was off and running.

CHAPTER TWO

From the West

The first Pony Express rider from the West was to start April 3 from Sacramento. But the ceremonial send-off for him was to be held in San Francisco. The San Franciscans had fought a long while for better mail service and, now that it was here, they wanted to celebrate it.

San Francisco had begun as a little Mexican village known as Buena Yerba, which means "good herb" and is thought to refer to the profusion of wild mint in the area. On February 2, 1846, following the Mexican-American War, California was ceded to the United States. At that time, Buena Yerba became San Francisco.

At first the town was just a little frontier trading post for furs brought down from Canada. Situated on a natural harbor, the location and mild climate made San

The booming city of San Francisco in the late 1850s. *(Library of Congress)*

Francisco an ideal trading site. But in January of 1848, gold was discovered nearby, and by 1849, the gold rush was in full swing. People flocked to the new territory in droves—so many, in fact, that just one year later California was given statehood.

By the mid-1850s, San Francisco had become one of the largest and wealthiest cities in America. A sprawl of modest houses spilled out from the city's center, among them a number of fine-looking mansions. The dirt streets of the downtown area were lined with several elegant hotels and theaters where outstanding performers from the East were booked. The city had acquired an air of polish, but it was only a thin veneer overlying the rip-roaring spirit of the gold rush era.

The Pony Express's promise of challenge and danger

stirred this adventurous spirit to a fever pitch. Those who could afford the cost wrote letters to be carried east. Eighty-five pieces of mail were quickly collected even though the price was steep: five dollars a half-ounce. (Later, the amount was reduced to one dollar a half-ounce.)

Early on the morning of April 3, people began gathering for the show. By early afternoon, dense crowds were already packing the route the pony and rider would follow. Shortly before four o'clock, young James Randall led a palomino pony out of the Alta Telegraph premises. The pony was beautiful to look at but not the caliber of animal required by the Pony Express. That didn't matter because pony and rider were both there just for show. And showy the little pony was, glittering with silver trappings from which dozens of small American flags fluttered.

Because the Pony Express would really depart from Sacramento, a stand-in was used for a real rider. James Randall looked resplendent in brand-new buckskins ornamented with fringes and silver studs. Those who were well acquainted with the frontier knew that no true frontiersman would handicap himself with so much excess weight.

The crowd cheered as an attendant brought out a saddle embossed with silver and placed it on the pony. Then came the mochila. The large lettering on it read OVERLAND PONY EXPRESS. The leather boxes that dangled from its four corners contained the eighty-five letters San Franciscans had written.

Despite James Randall's handsome appearance and fine outfit, he was obviously no true horseman. He tried to mount from the wrong side. Finally, Randall got himself astride the pony to a burst of cheers. Settling himself into the saddle and putting his feet in the stirrups, he gave a quick flick of his quirt and redeemed his clumsy mounting efforts by sending the pony off at a gallop.

Pony and rider raced down the crowd-lined streets to the riverfront. There, a steamer, the *Antelope,* was waiting. The mochila containing the letters was lifted from the pony and carried aboard the ship, which then sailed away. There is no further record of what happened to Randall and the pony. It is possible they also went aboard only to be put ashore a short distance upstream where their departure wouldn't be noticed. Or perhaps they just walked away.

With the mochila aboard, the *Antelope* continued upstream. Ten hours later, it dropped anchor at its mooring place outside Sacramento. It was two o'clock in the morning. The wharf was almost deserted except for a rider, young William (Billy) Hamilton, who was waiting there with his horse. He was accompanied by a representative from the Sacramento office of the Pony Express. That man accepted the mochila from the *Antelope.* He placed it on the saddle of Hamilton's horse and then put the letters from Sacramento in the mochila mailboxes and locked them.

Now all was ready. Hamilton mounted and set off through the pouring rain. Underfoot, the soaked ground

The famous side-wheeler *Antelope* could often be found in the bustle of the Sacramento waterfront, shown here in this late-1850s painting. *(Museum of Fine Arts, Boston)*

was slippery. The trail was hard to find and follow in the darkness. The rider pressed on through the rain-scoured night, stopping only to change horses at the stations along the way.

Six forty-five in the morning found Hamilton arriving at the gold mining town of Placerville. Despite the darkness, the rain, the faint trail, the steady uphill climb into the towering Sierra Nevada range, it had taken him only four hours to cover forty-five miles. He was half an hour ahead of schedule. Changing horses for the last time, Hamilton set off for his final stop—Sportsman's Hall, twelve miles distant. Young Warren Upson was waiting there to receive the mochila and be on his way into the very heart of the Sierras. The Pony Express had to cover close to 2,000 miles. Upson was to face one of the biggest challenges of the route.

Upson was the son of the editor of the *Sacramento*

Union. He had already tried his luck at mining in the silver and gold fields around Carson City on the other side of the mountains. But no amount of precious ore could hold him to the dark underground world of the mines. He had given it up for work with horses on California ranches and days of hunting in the Sierra Nevadas. He knew these mountains well.

Sierra Nevada is Spanish for "snowy range," but it is also referred to as the Range of Light because of the mountains' distinctive light-colored rock. Named by a Spanish explorer in 1776, the Sierras stretch four hundred miles from north to south through California, ranging in height from 9,000 feet to about 13,000. The highest point in the continental United States is the Sierras' Mount Whitney. Upson was headed for a pass near Lake Tahoe, one of the lower elevations.

As he rode upward, Upson encountered snow flurries that eventually became a blizzard. A freezing wind bearing down from the Arctic was flinging itself in wild gusts against rider and mustang. Already, deep snowdrifts had blanketed the slopes.

Because of the weather, the usual procession of wagons, mules, and horsemen carrying goods to Carson City was not around. And the trail that Upson knew so well was now buried under snowdrifts. The sturdy little mustang had to break its own trail. Sometimes when it began to flounder, Upson would dismount and take the lead, stamping out a trail for the mustang to follow.

Compared to the tall handsome thoroughbreds of the

East, the mustang of the West was a thin, wiry horse. But western riders quickly learned of the mustang's amazing endurance and ability to forage for food in barren land. A hardy mustang was just the horse a Pony Express rider needed to help him across the vast expanses of the West.

Upson's trail wound around the southern tip of Lake Tahoe and then turned down. At the Pony Express station in Genoa, Upson traded his weary mustang for a fresh mount and rode on. With his descent the snowdrifts had been dwindling. The sleet changed to rain, then to drizzle, and finally he was riding through afternoon sunlight. It was late when Upson finally reached Carson City. He had covered more than a hundred miles in twelve hours and was ready for a good meal and a well-earned rest.

The mochila continued on through the desert lands of what is today Nevada, passing from horse to horse and, less frequently, from rider to rider. All around them, the great platter of desert shimmered under the April sun. The open expanse was broken occasionally by tree-clad mountain chains with their tantalizing promise of cool green woodlands. But the riders had no time to stop to rest. They stuck to the trail that ran through scatterings of desert scrub or over sheets of alkali where nothing grew, and the glittering expanse burned their eyes.

As the day warmed, horses and men began to sweat profusely while the monotony of those long empty spaces brought on drowsiness. It was easy for the riders, secure in the saddle, to doze off, letting the reins droop

Opposite: The snowy and treacherous Sierra Nevada. *(Library of Congress)*

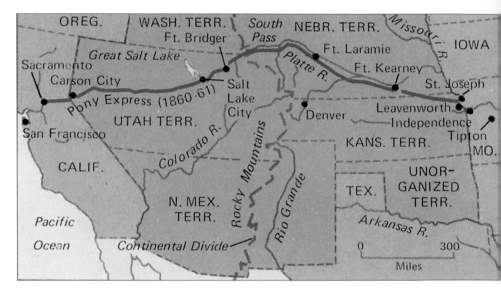

The Pony Express route, stretching from St. Joseph, Missouri, to Sacramento, California.

slack in their hands—a costly error during the first run of the Pony Express. Until the horses knew that the route would eventually lead them to food and water, they would be tempted to wander off the trail in search of both. By the time some jolt or other wakened the rider, he might find himself well off the trail in an empty expanse without any clues to guide him back.

Blinding dust storms sometimes whipped across the land, drowning everything in a stinging fog of sharp-edged grit that clogged eyes, nostrils, and throats, and hid the trail. When this happened, desert travelers usually hunkered down and waited for the storm to pass. But the tight schedule of the Pony Express didn't allow for this luxury, so the mustang had to be trusted to keep to the path.

The rainstorms that hit the desert, sometimes with little warning, were another danger. Rolling thunder followed crackling lightning before the sky unleashed a sudden cloud burst. The formerly dry creek beds would suddenly flood with water, and freshets would rush down every incline, the torrent so swift the mustang and its rider could be swept away.

But no crisis seems to have troubled the riders on the first Pony Express run. They raced unchallenged across the empty basin, passing the mochila from station to station, forty-seven of them in all, strung like beads across the desert floor. The last rider on the desert run headed toward the scalloped silhouette of the Ruby Mountain range that formed the western boundary of the Great Salt Lake Valley.

When dust storms struck the barren Nebraska desert, there were very few places for a Pony Express rider to take shelter. *(Library of Congress)*

The rider followed the trail into pleasant Ruby Valley, lying like a jewel in the heart of the mountains. Strewn with small lakes and ponds, green with vegetable gardens and open meadows where cattle grazed, it was a welcome sight. Here the rider would remain, sleeping, eating, and waiting until the returning mochila sent him flying back along the way he had come.

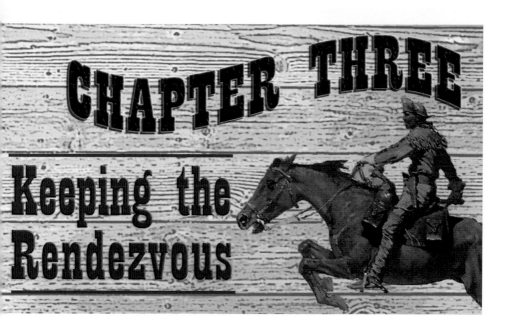

CHAPTER THREE

Keeping the Rendezvous

It would take several riders to carry the mochila east over the difficult jumble of the Ruby Mountains and on into the Great Salt Lake Valley. Each rider would cover seventy-five miles and would have five horse changes. The men assigned to the task were already well acquainted with the treacherous trail they would have to follow, so it was no surprise to them to see the telltale signs of an approaching storm. As the first rider set out, the wind was gathering strength, sending the black clouds scudding across the sky over the mountains. By the time the rider reached Butte station, flurries of snow had begun to fall.

Beyond Butte, the trail continued to mount upward. As horse and rider pressed forward into the storm, snowfall became heavier and was mingled with sleet.

This 1866 painting by Albert Bierstadt, entitled *Storm in the Rocky Mountains,* depicts the drama with which clouds could gather and let loose in the mountainous regions of the West. *(The Brooklyn Museum, New York)*

Driven by a wind now at gale force, icy needles stung the faces of man and animal. Underfoot patches of ice made the horse's hooves skid. The rider, trusting to his mustang, continued on. Rider after rider following the ridges of canyons always pressed forward.

The high point of the trail was at the head of Egan Canyon, which led down into the Great Salt Lake Valley. The canyon was named after Major Howard Egan, a prominent figure in Salt Lake City. Brigham Young, the leader of the large Mormon settlements in Utah, had given Major Egan the chore of mapping out the quickest route from the Great Salt Lake Valley to Sacramento. This route, which was currently being followed by the Pony Express riders, ran through the canyon now named after him.

Beyond the Pony Express stop at Egan Station, the trail continued its torturous descent, sometimes following the brink of canyons, sometimes descending into cramped valleys. One by one the riders passed through a string of these stations—Shell, Owl, Spring Valley, Antelope Valley, Deep Creek—changing horses at each. Night had descended by the time the mochila was turned over to William Fisher at Fish Springs. He was to ride the seventy-mile stretch to Rush Valley, which marked the end of his lap.

As Fisher approached Rush Valley, every station where he stopped to exchange horses reported that a major storm was still lashing the valley. Creeks and rivulets were overflowing their banks, and there were flash floods everywhere. If the way to Salt Lake City had been made so impassable that a relief rider couldn't make it through to Rush Valley, Fisher would feel honor bound to try to get the mochila to Salt Lake City himself. He dreaded the thought of the seventy-five extra miles he would still have to travel that night, much of it through the same wild canyon country he had just covered.

Pony Express rider Billy Fisher.

But as Fisher rode onto the station grounds, he saw waiting for him the straight-backed silhouette of Major Howard Egan himself. Like Fisher, he had been worried by the sudden onslaught of bad weather. Not wanting to jeopardize the final stretch of the Pony Express's first run, he had decided to carry the mochila to Salt Lake City himself.

As Fisher transferred the pouch, he saw that the major's mount was a fiery spirited stallion of which many stories were told. It was said the horse would obey its master's every

Major Howard Egan. *(Library of Congress)*

command without hesitation, while refusing to be mounted by anyone else. If any horse could make it through the flooded valley, this one could, leaving Fisher to relax, enjoy a hearty meal, and get a good night's sleep.

Major Egan and his horse were quickly on their way eastward. The path was as treacherous as Fisher had imagined it would be. In the blackness there were places where Egan could not even see the road. In stretches, it was slippery with liquid mud, causing the horse's hooves to skid.

The horse managed well until it reached the wooden bridge that crossed Mill River. There it came to an abrupt halt, for the bridge was awash with swirling water. Egan shouted encouragement and finally got the horse moving again. Midway across the bridge, the horse slipped on a thin sheet of mud that the water had deposited on the bridge's wooden planks. The animal struggled to retain its balance but failed.

Over it plunged into the swollen river, Major Egan still astride its back. For a few seconds the horse floundered in the rushing current, fighting to keep from being swept downstream. Then it found its footing and worked its way to the far bank. Struggling up the muddy slope, it finally stood again on solid ground.

Horse and rider, drenched and shivering, raced on. By 11:45 PM, they clattered into Salt Lake City. At the Pony Express office, young William Dennis was waiting to carry the mochila on to the rendezvous with the rider

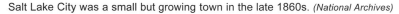

Salt Lake City was a small but growing town in the late 1860s. *(National Archives)*

from the East. By this time the storm was fading away. Snow and sleet had dwindled to drizzle. The wind was dying down. Egan, sure that the path ahead was not likely to pose any serious problems, relinquished the mochila to Dennis.

The young man set out at once, leaving Salt Lake City behind. By the time he had reached the rendezvous point, the clouds had cleared and stars appeared. So far, the Pony Express had proved its worth. Despite storms, floods, snow, and sleet, the riders from the West had kept to their schedule. But the pride Dennis felt over this feat quickly faded to worry as the other rider failed to arrive from the East.

Time kept ticking away. Minutes passed into hours.

Thomas Owen King. *(Church of Jesus Christ of Latter-day Saints)*

Hour after hour went slipping by. Almost nineteen hours late, the rider from the East finally arrived. Thomas Owen King explained that the trail had been bogged down with storms, blizzards, flooding rivers, and quagmires. Rider after rider had to struggle against almost impossible odds, losing precious time along the way. Now only the skill and speed of the returning riders could make up for the lost time.

Dennis and King exchanged mochilas and were soon galloping back along the trail over which they had just come. Riding through bright sunlight, Thomas Owen King was thankful for the change of weather. His way now led through the fifteen miles of trail that threaded Echo Valley, the eastern exit to the Great Salt Lake Valley. Beyond it stretched a jumble of steep canyons and intervening ridges. For most of the way, the trail followed the tops of these ridges.

It was twenty miles out of Echo Valley that King's luck changed. He ran into a blinding storm. Rain cascaded over the narrow trail. The horse stumbled on the slippery track and threw King. The mochila went sailing over a cliff.

Drenched by the cold rain and shivering, King clam-

The Pony Express station at Fort Bridger. *(Library of Congress)*

bered down the steep face of the cliff. He found the mochila and made his way back to the horse. Once more they were on their way, arriving at Fort Bridger thoroughly drenched but, at least, with no more time lost.

Just beyond Fort Bridger, King came to the end of his run. He had reached the place where two trails forked. The one King had been following out of the Great Salt Lake Valley was known as the Mormon Trail. It had been blazed by Mormon pioneers who had settled in the valley. The other trail led northward. It was the Oregon Trail, followed by pioneers heading for the green lands of Oregon and northern California. Beyond the fork the two trails gradually melted into one.

Later in the month the trail would have been clogged by a steady procession of covered wagons, horses, cattle, people, and even dogs. The Pony Express riders would

The Oregon Trail, stretching from Independence, Missouri, to Oregon City, is marked here in red. The trail to California, marked in yellow, forks off near Fort Hall.

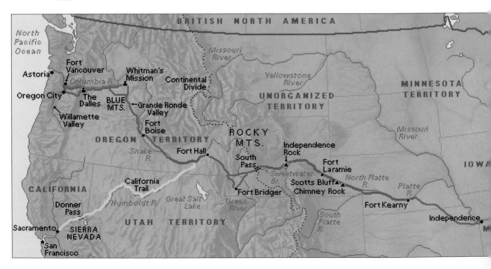

Hundreds of wagons make their way through South Pass, a valley near Fort Bridger. South Pass marked the halfway point for those traveling the Oregon Trail, but the hardest part of the journey, through the mountains, was still to come. *(Utah Historical Society)*

have to thread their way through all these travelers. But it was still very early in April, and most of the wagon trains didn't set out until the end of the month or even early May to avoid as much bad weather as possible. This meant that on their first run, the Pony Express riders would have an open road. Beyond Fort Bridger the trail ran across the high plateau country of southern Wyoming and into the swelling buttresses of the Rocky Mountains. Like a massive spine, this great range divides the eastern United States from the western United States.

The Pony Express rider headed up into South Pass. At this time of year South Pass is often buffeted by fierce blizzards. But no matter what kind of weather the riders faced, one after the other they raced on, determined to make up for lost time.

From South Pass, the trail led down the gentle eastern slopes, passing little Fort Laramie on the way. It was the last of several small army outposts in the western territories. At the foot of the Rockies, the trail wound through a burnt-orange land of mesas, buttes, and weird rock formations. Then turning southward, it entered northern Colorado and headed for the town of Julesburg, perched on the southern bank of the Platte River.

That lap's rider, James Moore, would have to cross the broad Platte to follow the trail. The Platte was usually a shallow ford. But on that day recent rains and melting snows had turned it into a raging torrent. As Moore neared the river, curious crowds began to gather on the far bank. They wanted to see how a rider of the

During the late winter and early spring, wagon trains and lone riders had a very difficult time crossing the wide waters of the Platte.

Pony Express would fare at the dangerous crossing.

Moore didn't hesitate. He urged his mount into the racing current. A sudden surge struck full force against the horse, throwing it off balance. It floundered, thrashing and kicking while Moore tried vainly to get it back on its feet. But the current was too strong. It swept horse and rider downstream. A short distance farther on, the horse became mired in a patch of quicksand.

Moore leapt from the horse and snatched up the mochila. Holding it high above his head, he waded thigh deep through the freezing water and scrambled up the far bank. Spotting a man astride a horse, he commandeered the animal. He threw the mochila over its back and leapt into the saddle. Off he rode to the huddle of shanties that was Julesburg. At the Pony Express station there, he passed the mochila on to the next rider. Then he raced back to return the borrowed horse and claim his own, which the helpful crowd had already rescued. Only then was a drenched and freezing Moore free to turn in for a much-needed rest.

Beyond Julesburg, the trail led through the almost-treeless prairies of Nebraska. The water-soaked land was a maze of wandering rivulets, marshes, and sinkholes. Horse and rider had to keep a close lookout. A single misstep could cause the horse to stumble, throw the rider, and injure both, delaying the mochila.

Finally, horse and rider reached Fort Kearny. Beyond the little trading post and fort, the prairies began to give way to cultivated fields. Groves of trees started to appear. Small villages, some only tiny settlements, lined the trail. The way became easier now. The riders raced along, eating up the miles. By noon on the thirteenth of April, the last rider arrived at Seneca and handed the mochila over to Billy Richardson. Richardson had made the first run here. Now he would carry the mochila back to St. Joseph.

Urging his horse on, Richardson arrived at the Elwood ferry crossing at 9:30 PM on April 13. The lost time had been made up. The mail was on schedule. Richardson and his horse were carried across the Missouri River. Then they were off again, galloping into St. Joseph.

By the time Richardson arrived, the hour was late but the town's folk were all out to greet him. Members of the local militia, in hastily donned uniforms, were parading up and down the streets, stopping now and then to fire their muskets into the air. Kindling of all kinds had been heaped at the street corners and set afire.

Richardson rode through the town to the Patee House, and the cannon that had boomed to send him on his way roared again to welcome him back. Church bells rang and fire stations clanged their anvils.

The mayor, who had been reelected during Richardson's brief absence, spoke in praise of the successful run of the Pony Express. As the crowd went off to bed, the firm's owners, Russell, Majors, and Waddell, still had their worries. The run east had been successful. But there was still no telling how the run westward to Sacramento had fared. Once rider and horse had left the Great Salt Lake Valley, no news was heard of them.

CHAPTER FOUR

Success

William Dennis had carried the mochila to Salt Lake City, where he handed it over to an anxious Erastus "Ras" Egan. After a brief explanation for his delayed arrival, Dennis sent Ras on his way. Ras was taking more than the mochila with him—he also carried a warning from his father, Major Howard Egan, who had just received word from several of the army posts scattered throughout the West: the Paiute and Shoshone tribes with some other tribes were becoming more and more hostile to the increasing numbers of intruders into their regions. The threat of war was in the air. Ras was to see that this warning was passed along from rider to rider and station to station. All should be on the alert for suspicious movements in their area.

Reaching Rush Valley, Ras passed the mochila on to

his friend William Fisher, who then started retracing his way westward, this time in bright sunshine. All along the way he kept an eye out for any ambush that might lurk for him there. But neither Fisher nor the succession of riders that took the mochila on encountered any such attacks. Good weather

Major Egan's son, "Ras" Egan.

was helping them all make up the time lost by the eastern riders.

Soon, the last rider had made his way through the barrier mountains and into Ruby Valley. From there the chain of riders, passing the mochila and the warning along, raced through the Nevada desert. Day and night, they scanned the distant horizons for any sign of warriors on the move. But all they saw now and then was the silhouette of a solitary figure sitting motionless astride his horse—watching but making no further move.

At every station, the riders passed along the warning that Major Egan had issued. But the managers of the stations only shrugged. They said they had had no indication of any real trouble. They had been carefully following the advice they had been given when they were first hired. They showed only friendliness and good will toward the Paiutes who sometimes came visiting. They had little reason to fear their Native American neighbors.

The station managers reassured the riders and were also able to cast light on the lonely watchers they had been seeing along the way. Visiting Paiutes had brought up the subject which had been troubling them ever since the first run of the Pony Express. They wanted to know why the rider was in such haste and what was in that strange-looking leather pouch. Did it contain some potent magic? No denials by the station managers could calm their anxiety. They were determined to get their hands on that pouch to investigate its contents.

The riders realized that even the lonely watchers whom they had been taking for granted could be a source of trouble. They knew that if any of the watchers started to move toward them, they would be wise to speed away in the opposite direction. But their chief concern was still to make up for lost time and get the mail in on schedule.

The riders went long stretches completely alone. They saw little wildlife—now and then a hare would leap away from the horse's hooves, and sometimes the harsh rattle of a rattlesnake preparing to strike would warn horse and rider to veer from their course. The black buzzards circling overhead would reveal the presence of some small dying creature in the scrub below.

Night brought on the freezing chill of a desert spring. In the dark sky, streams of stars revolved over the riders' heads. Underfoot there was only the scurrying and rustling of small desert creatures—mice, lizards, and rats.

Two-thirds of the way across the desert, the rider reached Cold Springs station. Beyond that station the trail entered dense thickets of sagebrush. Many of the plants grew so high a horse could have moved through them unseen and unheard. The only sound was the rustle of wind in the sagebrush and the melancholy baying of distant coyotes.

Ambush would be easy in this place. The rider would have to depend on the mustang for a timely warning. He focused his eyes on the horse's ears. He knew that if any danger threatened, those sensitive ears would prick up nervously. But the ears stayed relaxed, and presently the rider coming out of the sagebrush thickets reached the Sand Springs station.

There was no need to worry about ambush here. The land wore a coverlet of shimmering white alkali on which nothing could grow. Over the glistening expanse the rider galloped, past clusters of high pale sand dunes and on to the Carson Sink. The sink was a hollow depression where the Carson River, fed by melting snows, spread out to form small lakes interspersed with soggy marshes. Trailblazers for the Pony Express had laid down a rough road over the worst of the marshes.

This painting by Frederic Remington, entitled *The Coming and Going of the Pony Express,* embodies much of the romance and excitement associated with the Pony Express. *(The Thomas Gilcrease Institute of American History and Art, Tulsa, OK)*

It was made of rows of willow logs. Over them the horse's hooves beat a steady tattoo as it raced toward its final stop, Carson City.

At Carson City, Warren Upson was waiting to take the mochila again. By this time the storm had spent itself. The snowdrifts still remained, but the trail itself had been cleared. The ascent was easy until daylight returned. Then the trail became crowded with slow-moving mule trains hauling wagons filled with supplies for Carson City. At times traffic so clogged the road that Upson was unable to weave through it. Once again, the mustang had to leave the trail and plough through the drifts that lined it.

After rounding Lake Tahoe, horse and rider started on

Snowstorms caused significant perils and delays for stagecoaches and riders crossing through the Sierras. *(The Thomas Gilcrease Institute of American History and Art, Tulsa, OK)*

the downward stretch. At one o'clock in the afternoon, they reached Sportsman's Lodge, where William Hamilton was waiting to take the mochila on to Sacramento. When Hamilton had started his run east ten days ago, he had left Sacramento in the dead of night, alone and unsung. But now the news of his arrival had preceded him. At Placerville he found a crowd led by the mayor himself waiting to greet him. Accompanied by shouts and cheers, the mayor escorted Hamilton through the town and saw him off.

Sacramento was ready to give him a proper welcome too. Already flags were flying above public buildings. Merchants had decorated the windows of their shops with great signs that read HURRAH FOR THE CEN-

TRAL ROUTE! And crowds were gathering along the road Hamilton would follow on his ride into town.

An escort had already ridden out to Sutter's Fort to greet Hamilton. As they returned with him in tow, a cannon began to boom. It fired off forty rounds before it fell silent. Fire engine anvils clanged. Riding through all the hubbub, Hamilton reached the Pony Express office at 5:25 PM, April 13. Hamilton had almost brought the mail in on schedule—he was just two minutes late. While Hamilton went off for a well-deserved rest, the Pony Express superintendent sorted the mail. The letters for San Francisco were returned to the mochila, which was placed on a fresh horse. The horse and another rider boarded the waiting *Antelope*. The little paddle steamer put on all speed and reached San Francisco at half-past midnight.

Despite the lateness of the hour, the arrival of the steamer was greeted with clanging bells. People lined Montgomery Street, where bonfires blossomed at intervals. As

Once the Pony Express had completed a successful run, advertisements and promotions for the service sprang up around the country.

PONY EXPRESS !

CHANGE OF TIME!   REDUCED RATES!

10 Days to San Francisco!

LETTERS

WILL BE RECEIVED AT THE

OFFICE, 84 BROADWAY,

NEW YORK,

Up to 4 P. M. every TUESDAY,

AND

Up to 2½ P. M. every SATURDAY,

Which will be forwarded to connect with the PONY EXPRESS leaving ST. JOSEPH, Missouri,

Every WEDNESDAY and SATURDAY at 11 P. M.

TELEGRAMS

Sent to Fort Kearney on the evenings of MONDAY and FRIDAY, will connect with PONY leaving St. Joseph, WEDNESDAYS and SATURDAYS.

EXPRESS CHARGES.

LETTERS weighing half ounce or under............$1 00
For every additional half ounce or fraction of an ounce 1 00
In all cases to be enclosed in 10 cent Government Stamped Envelopes,
And all Express CHARGES Pre-paid.

PONY EXPRESS ENVELOPES For Sale at our Office.

WELLS, FARGO & CO., Ag'ts.

New York, Jn'y 1, 1861.

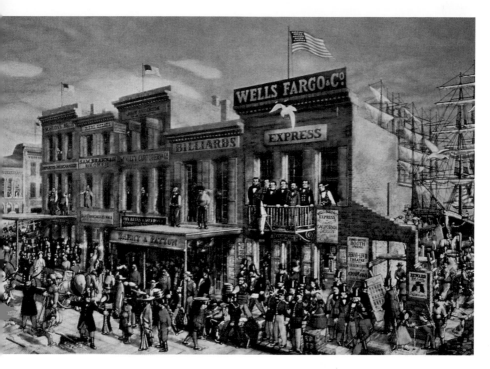

Crowds await the first delivery of Pony Express mail on San Francisco's bustling Montgomery Street. *(Wells Fargo Bank History Room)*

rider and pony came ashore, a band struck up "Hail the Conquering Hero Comes." Local fire engines, men on horseback, and others on foot marched down the street escorting the bulging mochila to the Alta Telegraph office.

When word of the successful westward run by the Pony Express reached St. Joseph, the whole country went mad. Newspapers heralded the achievements of the fabulous and glorious Pony Express. The story caught the imagination of the outside world as well. Newspapers everywhere marveled at how the huge North American continent had been spanned in just ten days' time by the efforts of a band of gallant youths. They had become the world's latest heroes.

CHAPTER FIVE

The Stations

The initial success of the Pony Express was largely due to good planning by its owners. They were quick to take advantage of those stagecoach stations already set up along part of the route. The stations were set seventy-five to one hundred miles apart and were used by stagecoach drivers to change their tired horses for fresh ones. The stops were also convenient for taking on or letting off passengers and picking up slow mail for delivery along the route.

When the Pony Express started using these stations, they added their own facilities. They had depots in which quantities of food and other necessities were stored to be distributed to the smaller relay stations as needed. There were corrals and stables for the horses, and barns to hold the supplies of hay needed to supplement any grazing they were able to do. It was from this central supply of horses that the small relay stations could replace any of their own horses that got sick or died.

This enabled the small stations to get along on a few horses and a skeleton crew, consisting of a manager and several stockmen. Rarely did a visitor stop at a relay station whose sole purpose was to service the Pony Express riders and their horses. Many of the larger stations were surrounded by a cluster of shops and services—blacksmiths, boot makers, leather workers, and carpenters. Some stations had their own hotels, owned and run by the station managers. The hotels were used by the Pony Express riders during their stopover periods.

Billy Richardson was probably the luckiest of the riders because he was assigned the Patee House as one of his two home bases. During his stopovers at St. Joseph he could enjoy the entertainments to be found in town. At the end of his outward lap, he could still count on a

The Pony Express stables in St. Joseph. *(Library of Congress)*

The stopover station in Hollenburg, Kansas, one of the first stops past Seneca. *(Library of Congress)*

pleasant rest period as he waited for the incoming mochila. That stopover station was in the town of Seneca. His lodging there was in a hotel run by John F. Smith. The hotel had a great reputation among travelers for being one of the best around. It was especially noted for the meals Mrs. Smith served and the public dance parties held in the ballroom.

Beyond Seneca, lodgings became simpler but were still pleasant, located as they were in the midst of rolling fields dotted with clusters of farmhouses and webbed with streams. The hotels were usually rough, one-story log buildings with hard-packed dirt floors. The living room also served as dining room. One or two hotels might have the luxury of small washrooms with a tin tub that could be filled with a meager quantity of hot water brought from the nearby kitchen. But most only offered sponge baths for their guests—a shelf holding a pitcher of water, a basin, and a towel. Visitors who wanted more had to take a cold dip in a nearby stream. Sleeping quarters were usually small dormitory-style rooms with bunks crowded closely together.

Because this whole area was more or less settled, and therefore considered relatively safe from the Sioux who lived nearby, the owner of a lodging house often brought his wife and children to live with him so they could help with the work. If the wife was a good cook, she became a celebrity among travelers, though there was nothing unusual about the meals she served. They were hearty meals—slabs of fatty bacon, hot rolls, and eggs, along with vegetables and fruit in season, provided by local gardens and orchards.

Sometimes the diners might be treated to beef or chicken. Wild turkeys or venison might be served on special occasions, but they weren't easy to come by since most of the game animals that had once thrived in the area had been either hunted down or driven out. Bison steak was considered a rare treat, though one visitor complained it was so tough it had to be lubricated with bacon grease just to swallow it. The farther west the trail ran, the more primitive the stations became. In some places the food was so old that a traveler could expect eggs green with age along with the moldering bread and bacon. Sleeping quarters were so cramped that they were reserved for women travelers. The men had to sleep in barns on hay pallets or outside during fair weather. Some

A dugout house on the open prairie of Nebraska, just north of the Kansas border. *(Nebraska State Historical Society)*

stations, like the one at Pole Creek just east of Julesburg, were dugouts carved into the hillsides.

Beyond the Rocky Mountains and approaching the Great Salt Lake Valley, the accommodations, though primitive, were clean and comfortable. Most of the lodgings belonged to Mormons, for this was Mormon country. Its center was the Great Salt Lake Valley. Once travelers reached it, they found living accommodations almost as good as those around St. Joseph. Fresh vegetables and fruit came straight from the gardens and orchards the settlers had wrested from the desert soil.

The bleakest of all the Pony Express stations lay beyond the Ruby Mountains, on the far side of pleasant Ruby Valley. Here the trail entered Nevada's Great Basin Desert. In this empty land the little relay station huts, built of sun-dried adobe bricks, stood out forlornly like wilting mushrooms. Even the few horses quartered there had a lean, dusty look about them. The cramped adobe

Fish Springs station, located just west of the Great Salt Lake in the Ruby Valley.
(Utah State Historical Society, Salt Lake City)

stables and makeshift corrals seemed flimsy enough to fly away with the next big windstorm.

The home stations were scarcely bigger. They had been hastily put together and were used mainly as stopping off places for the Pony Express. As miserable as the barns and corrals looked, they still dwarfed the cramped living quarters of the manager and his one- or two-man crew. Windows in the tiny huts were just open apertures that had to be boarded up during sand or rainstorms. Chairs were upended boxes. The table was several rude planks laid across other boxes. Day and night a battered old coffeepot containing a strong dark brew sat on the table, accompanied by several cups. The stock tenders' implements hung from nails pounded into the hard adobe walls—brushes, curry combs, manure forks, saddles. A small medicine chest stood on a shelf in a corner. It contained remedies for both horses and men—

In this 1859 drawing by artist Daniel A. Jenks, two men approach large green plants from the western Nevada desert, while behind them a wagon train makes its way across the desert flats. Like many travelers in the mid-1800s, Jenks and his party took several days to make the desert crossing. *(Library of Congress)*

liniment, turpentine, and castor oil.

The huts were too small for more than one person to move easily around in them. Sleeping there was out of the question for everyone. Station managers, horse trainers, riders, and any chance traveler all had to sleep outside. If the night was bright and clear, they rolled themselves up in blankets and slept in the open. But if a sand or rainstorm swept over the land, they took shelter in the storage barn where, squeezed together, they slept on the hay.

Once a month, mule trains hauled in supplies. There were no fresh vegetables or fruit. They couldn't have lasted in the desert heat. Tripe, smoked hams, and fatty

bacon slabs provided the meat dishes. Almost everything else came in bags—dried beans, dried fruit, potatoes, and flour. Along with the bags came big jugs of
molasses and jars of pickles cured in brine. Everything
was stored in the tiny hut, and a close lookout had to be
kept for hungry rodents.

Water was a problem. Sometimes the men would try
locating underground water by digging wells. But after
digging one or two hundred feet down and finding
nothing but dry earth, they gave that up and had to
depend on water hauled to the station in barrels. This
meant importing enough to provide a month's supply for
horses as well as for the relay stations' human needs.
With water so scarce, nothing more than a sponge bath
could be allowed for the men.

Everyone had to make do with the scant amount of

Diamond Springs Pony Express station in Nevada. *(Nevada Historical Society, Reno)*

water in the basin, which was replaced only after it became so thick with grime it had to be thrown out. Faces and hands got just one cursory dunk before they were dried off on the tattered remnant of a shirt that stood for a towel. Everyone was exceedingly careful because to run out of water here would be to court a cruel death.

Beyond the desert stations, conditions changed for the better. From Cold Spring station in the Carson Sink, log buildings again appeared along with fresh vegetables, eggs, chickens, and plenty of water. From then on, travelers and Pony Express riders could expect pleasant lodgings all the way to Sacramento.

Station managers and their stockmen were important to the running of the Pony Express and had to be chosen with care. The man put in charge of this was Benjamin F. Ficklin, a trusted member of the Russell, Majors & Waddell team. He was given the position of general supervisor. His job was to oversee the whole route and select the proper men to act as division superintendents. These men were to oversee things in their divisions and report to Ficklin if there were any problems.

The first division ran from St. Joseph, Missouri, to Fort Kearny, Nebraska Territory. Ficklin named A. E. Lewis to be division superintendent. The second division ran from Fort Kearny to Horseshoe station near South Pass in the Rocky Mountains. Ficklin chose Joseph A. Slade to be division superintendent there.

The third division, running from Horseshoe station to Salt Lake City, was given to James E. Bromley, while

Major Howard Egan was given the fourth division, from Salt Lake City to Roberts Creek station. Bolivar Roberts was named division superintendent of the area between Roberts Creek and Sacramento, California.

The division that had given Ficklin the most concern was the second division, from Fort Kearny to Horseshoe station. The area was primarily a wilderness of jumbled rock formations with a few green valleys watered by small streams or rivers. For years it had been a favorite refuge for bandits, murderers, and desperados of all kinds.

Jules Reni had been a longtime resident of the area. He owned a ranch and had founded the town of Julesburg that bore his name. He had assumed the position of manager over the Julesburg Pony Express station. But it soon became apparent to Ficklin that Old Jules, as he was called, was allowing his ranch to be used as a sanctuary for desperados. He was even suspected of being the leader of one of the gangs.

Under Reni's protection the whole area had become one of the most dangerous stretches along the Pony Express route. There were daily raids on stagecoaches and attacks on individual travelers. Murders were frequent occurrences. Ficklin knew a solitary Pony Express rider would be an easy target. He was determined to get the whole region cleaned up—a difficult job. He would have to find a man as tough as old Jules himself. He settled on Joseph A. Slade.

Slade, though ordinarily mild mannered, was easily roused to action and would then go to any extremes to

Joseph Slade, superintendent of the second division.

achieve his goal. As soon as he was given the position, he moved to Horseshoe station and immediately fired Reni from his position as station manager.

Reni was furious and planned revenge for what he considered an insult. He ambushed Slade and filled him with buckshot from his double-barreled shotgun. Ficklin went after Reni, found him, and ordered him hanged on the spot. Fortunately for Reni, friends arrived in time to cut him down and save his life. Meanwhile, Slade had the buckshot removed from his body. He gathered a posse of some five or six men and went after Reni. He captured the old man and killed him. He and his posse then tracked down all the desperados in the area that

Pony Express Trail: Eastern Leg

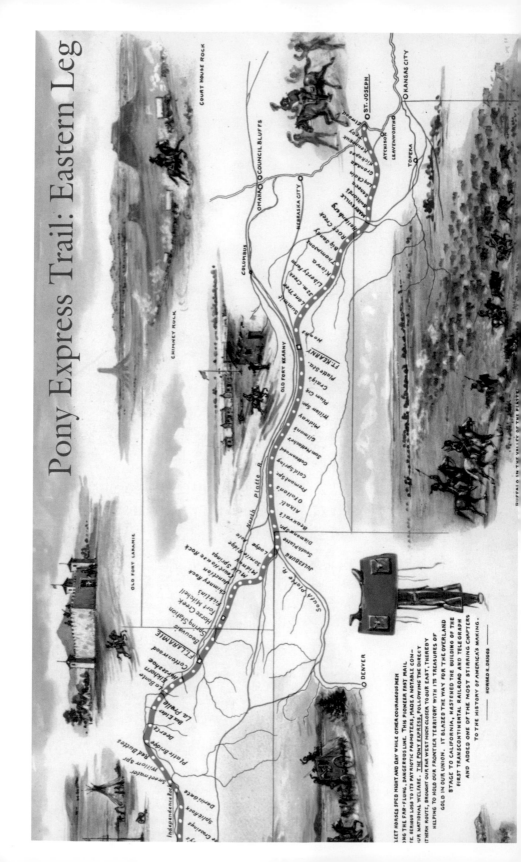

COURT HOUSE ROCK

CHIMNEY ROCK

OLD FORT LARAMIE

ST. JOSEPH

KANSAS CITY

LEAVENWORTH

Atchison
TOPEKA

Troy
Lincoln
Kennekuk
Granada
Log Chain
Seneca
Marysville
Guittard's
Cottonwood
Rock Creek
Big Sandy
Liberty Farm
Thompsons
Kiowa
32m. Creek
Lone Tree
Summit

OMAHA
COUNCIL BLUFFS
NEBRASKA CITY
COLUMBUS

Ho-kaws
FT. KEARNY
OLD FORT KEARNY
Platte Sta.
Plum Ck.
Craig's
Million Spr.
Midway
Gilmans
Sam Mochacks
Cottonwood
Cold Spring
Fremontspr.
O'Fallons
Alkali
Beauvois
Diamond Spr.
South Platte
JULESBURG

North Platte R.

South Platte R.

DENVER

Lodge Pole
Mud Springs
Junction
Chimney Rock
Ficklin's
Fort Mitchell
Horse Creek
Spring Station
Beauvais
FT. LARAMIE
Cottonwood
Ragasahoe
Bighorn
La Bonte
Deercr.
La Prelle
Box Elder
Platte Bridge
Millior spr.
Red Buttes
Sweetwater
Devils Gate
Independence Rock
Split Rock
Three Crossings

LEET HORSES SPED NIGHT AND DAY WHILE OTHER COURAGEOUS MEN
...NG THE FAR-FLUNG, DANGEROUS LINE. THIS PIONEER FAST MAIL
...E, SERIOUS LOSS TO ITS PATRIOTIC PROMOTERS, MADE A NOTABLE CON-
...OUR NATIONAL WELFARE. THE PONY EXPRESS, FOLLOWING THE DIRECT
...RTHERN ROUTE, BROUGHT OUR FAR WEST MUCH CLOSER TO OUR EAST, THEREBY
HELPING TO HOLD OUR FRONTIER TERRITORY WITH ITS TREASURES OF
GOLD IN OUR UNION. IT BLAZED THE WAY FOR THE OVERLAND
STAGE TO CALIFORNIA, HASTENED THE BUILDING OF THE
FIRST TRANSCONTINENTAL RAILROAD AND TELEGRAPH
AND ADDED ONE OF THE MOST STIRRING CHAPTERS
TO THE HISTORY OF AMERICA'S MAKING.

—— HOWARD R. DRIGGS ——

BUFFALO IN THE VALLEY OF THE PLATTE

Pony Express Trail: Western Leg

they could find and killed them too. By the time Slade was finished, he had earned a reputation for such ferocity that those who managed to escape his wrath fled the area, making it one of the safest stretches on the route.

Slade was only one of the many unique characters who worked for the Pony Express. With

"Wild Bill" Hickock. *(Library of Congress)*

its aura of romance and action, it attracted such colorful people as James Butler (Wild Bill) Hickock. The record is unclear about Hickock's service to the Pony Express, but he was probably too heavy to be a rider. If he worked at all for the Pony Express, it was as a stock tender at Rock Creek station. Hickock was famous for his gun-fighting skills.

History does report that when a violent quarrel broke out between the station manager and a man named McCanles and two of his friends, Hickock shot McCanles to death and wounded his two companions. Hickock was tried for murder but was acquitted. He went on to serve as a Union scout during the Civil War, and then as a peace officer in the wild cities of the West. He gained even more fame after touring with Buffalo Bill Cody and was eventually shot to death in an ambush in Deadwood, South Dakota.

Station managers came from all parts of the United States. Some were even immigrants from abroad. George Hollenberg, who managed the Cottonwood station in Kansas, was a German citizen. He had traveled the world, visiting California's gold rush towns before sailing off to Australia, which was also in its gold rush days. From Australia he sailed to Peru, finally ending up back in America. In Kansas, he purchased a ranch near the stagecoach and Pony Express route. He profited not only as a station manager but also as the owner of a popular hotel he had built there.

Several French Canadians had also crossed over the border to open ranches in areas around the Rocky Mountains, and some of them became station managers. The largest of these ranches was at Horseshoe station, where Slade made his headquarters.

The station at Three Crossings, located in the valley of the Sweetwater River west of the Rockies, was run by a Mr. and Mrs. Moore, an English couple. They had been converted to Mormonism when in England, and, filled with zeal, had traveled to America to join the Mormon settlement in the Great Salt Lake Valley. However, at Three Crossings, Mrs. Moore learned that many of the men in the valley practiced polygamy. Not wanting to

The Pony Express station at Three Crossings. *(St. Joseph Museum, St. Joseph)*

share her husband with other wives and afraid the temptation to do so might prove too strong for him, she insisted on settling at Three Crossings. The couple ran both a station and a small hostel for travelers passing through.

Once the Julesburg area had been cleaned up, the most dangerous stretch on the Pony Express route was located west of Salt Lake City. The jumbled Ruby Mountains had long been the home of the Paiutes, Shoshones, and other related tribes. There, the Humboldt River, flowing westward out of the mountains, had created an oasis along its short course into the desert.

This oasis was rich with game, seed grasses, and piñon trees that provided nuts the native women gathered and ground into flour, a basic food for them. But increasing numbers of covered wagons began following the Humboldt River, soiling its waters with animal droppings and other debris. The newcomers were cutting down the piñon trees for wood to repair their wagons. And they were either driving away or shooting the game.

Seeing the main sources of their food being destroyed, the Paiutes retaliated with sporadic attacks on the wagon trains. There was no way of knowing how they would react to the thinly manned Pony Express stations set up in this area. To lessen the danger, managers were chosen from among the Mormons who had been born and grown up in the valley. As children, they had made lasting friendships with the Paiutes. This knowledge would prove helpful in maintaining good relations with the tribes among whom they would be living.

The strangest men of all were the managers and stockmen who ran the stations in the desert west of Robert's Creek. Though these men were only in their late twenties or early thirties, their skin, made leathery by years of sun and windburn, was so creased with wrinkles they seemed much older than they were. Few were married, and those who were would never have thought of bringing their wives to these desolate expanses.

What housekeeping was done, the men did for themselves. The manager usually cooked the meals. His cooking skills were basic. He boiled the beans and the potatoes, fried the tripe, ham, and bacon, and stewed the dried fruit. In the adobe oven he baked loaves of bread by the dozen.

Habitual loners, the men didn't mind their solitary life. It was enough for them to get the periodic visits of the Pony Express riders who brought them the latest news from east and west. The monthly visits of the supply wagons loaded with provisions provided another break in the monotony of their everyday life. But what delighted the desert men most was the appearance of some bedraggled traveler at their door. The men welcomed such visitors wholeheartedly, treating them with what food and drink they had. Far into the night, guest and hosts would squat over cups of stale syrupy black coffee and, through clouds of rank tobacco smoke, regale one another with fantastic tales of past adventures, mostly spun from fertile imaginations.

Whether they were entertaining visitors or just enjoying the desert silences, the men all shared one thing in common—the vast distances that lay between them and help of any kind, should the need arise. In this empty desert, his only protection a rifle, each man at his station was terribly vulnerable to trouble.

CHAPTER SIX
The Riders

The first run of the Pony Express riders was followed by many more, all keeping so close to schedule that Russell pressured his more conservative partners to make the run twice instead of once weekly. This meant that riders used to having six days of leisure between runs were now limited to one day and night. The quickened pace put a strain on them physically and emotionally. Very few riders lasted the whole eighteen months the Pony Express was in operation.

One of the first to leave was Alex Carlyle, a young man with a persistent cough that had been diagnosed as tuberculosis. He had hoped that the exercise and fresh air he would get working for the Pony Express would cure him. Instead he became so ill he had to resign and find a less stressful job.

Other riders left for different reasons. Sometimes it was a serious injury, sometimes a desire to marry and raise a family. Other times it was just the sheer boredom of doing run after run over the same ground once the initial excitement had worn off. But their leaving was no problem for the division superintendents, who had little trouble getting new recruits, such was the continuing glamour of the Pony Express.

Those who were chosen to work for the Pony Express were generally well equipped to handle the many problems they had to face. Most of the riders had spent their childhoods on the frontier where they had grown familiar with the native tribes living in their vicinity.

One of these riders was fifteen-year-old William Frederick Cody, who later achieved fame as Buffalo Bill. As a child in Kansas, Cody had learned the art of riding and shooting at the same time from the Kikapoo people, with whom he had developed a warm friendship.

Bill Cody at age fifteen, during the time he worked as a Pony Express rider.

Because of his skills, Cody was chosen to make the run from Red Buttes to Three Crossings, a dangerous area at the time. On his first run there, he found that the rider to whom he was to pass on the mochila had been killed. Without worrying about his own safety, Cody immediately mounted a fresh horse and raced on to Rocky Ridge station, where he handed

A poster promoting Buffalo Bill's Wild West show, featuring a Pony Express rider.

the mochila to the waiting rider and then raced back to Red Buttes. He had covered 360 miles without a rest.

Besides skillful horsemanship, young riders raised on the frontier had learned many valuable lessons from nature. Most important was the ability to read the secret clues it left, clues that no city-bred boy would have noticed. Sometimes that skill made the difference between life and death. One winter's day, eighteen-year-old William Campbell, riding westward from Fort Kearny, encountered a driving snowstorm. Drift piled upon drift until the whole prairie was blanketed with three to five feet of snow. In the summer, this section of prairie was covered with tall, tough grass, three to six feet high. The trail running through this grass forest could be plainly seen. The grass had died in the fall, but the straight brown stalks had continued to stand. Only their dry brown tips were visible above the blanket of snow, dotting the landscape everywhere.

As Campbell's eyes focused on them, he became suddenly aware of a pattern. Two parallel rows of tips marched purposefully across the plain and on to the horizon. Campbell realized that the hidden trail lay between those two rows. Thousands of wagon wheels, hooves of horses and oxen, and the heavy boots of human beings had worn away all the grass to create the trail.

Another time, a sudden thunderstorm overtook Campbell at nightfall. In the blackness that surrounded him he could see nothing underfoot. Sound alone guided

This drawing from *Hutchings* magazine (July 1860) depicts a Pony Express rider crossing a swollen and dangerous stream. *(California State Library)*

him to the bank of the Platte River, its waters roaring at flood strength. He knew the trail ran along the riverbank, but since he could not see in which direction the current was flowing, he did not know whether to follow the river to the left or to the right. So he tossed one end of his lariat into the water, holding the other end tightly. Once it hit the water, the lariat immediately pulled in the direction of the current.

Reading the clues left by nature didn't always work because nature can sometimes be a fickle guide. On a ride from Fort Crittenden to Rush Valley, Ras Egan was afraid he would lose direction when a heavy snowfall blanketed all his navigational clues. Before his departure from Fort Crittenden, Egan had learned that the wind was blowing from the north. So he turned his head from side to side until he felt the wind blowing against his right cheek. By keeping the wind on his right cheek, Egan was sure he was headed west.

Doggedly, his horse plodded on through the drifts only to find itself back at Fort Crittenden again. Midway to Rush Valley, the wind had suddenly veered and had begun to blow from the opposite direction. Egan just picked a fresh mount and started out again. By the time he reached Rush Valley he had covered one hundred and fifty miles through heavy snows and had still arrived on time.

Sometimes a rider's bulldog determination to keep the mail going almost cost him his life, as was the case with William Fisher. Fisher was doing a lap from Rush Valley to Salt Lake City when a heavy blizzard struck. He urged his horse into the darkening twilight and presently came to a small camp set up by a stagecoach driver who planned to wait out the night and be on his way the next day, when the trail was clear. But Fisher, his schedule in mind, set off into the storm.

Soon the falling curtains of snow were choking the narrow canyons that ran like ribs through the foothills into the valley. Pushing forward, Fisher suddenly realized he was hopelessly lost. Up and down he wandered, through canyon after canyon, trying to find his way through stands of cedar and juniper shrouded with snow. At last, completely confused and worn out, he decided on a short rest for both himself and his weary horse. He dismounted and turned his horse's back to the wind. Then he sat down, propped against the trunk of a cedar, for what he expected to be a brief rest.

Fisher was soon sinking into a sleep so deep he would probably never have awakened but for a jackrabbit. Hopping energetically across his knees, the rabbit startled

Both horse and rider battle exhaustion during one of the brutal western blizzards that challenged the Pony Express. *(California Historical Society, San Francisco)*

Fisher awake. Deciding to give his horse the lead, Fisher set out once more, plodding beside it in an effort to keep awake by exercising.

Fisher soon realized that allowing the horse its lead was a wise choice. The horse brought him unerringly to the banks of the River Jordan. Fisher, now knowing where he was, followed the river to the little town of Lehi, where he and his horse were welcomed and fed. Confident once more, Fisher mounted his horse and set off for Salt Lake City. But in the black snow-clad world, he lost his way again. As his horse wandered aimlessly through the heavy snowdrifts, a light ahead suddenly caught Fisher's eye. He directed his horse toward it. As he drew closer he saw that the light was shining from a window in a small house.

Leaving his worn-out horse to follow at its own slow pace, he pushed on. As he approached the small cabin, the people inside rushed out to welcome him. Several men hurried off to bring in his horse while the women led Fisher into the house and fed him a warm supper. After the horse had been fed and given time to rest, the men gave him directions for reaching the trail to Salt Lake City. This time Fisher found it without any problem.

All the Pony Express riders recognized that their success was due to more than their own ability to ride, to decipher nature's secret clues, and to their determination to get the mail through on time. It was also due to the sense of loyalty the Pony Express riders felt toward one another. They formed a close brotherhood that led them to step in and help out a fellow rider even if it meant adding miles to their own laps. Some, like Ras Egan and William Fisher, who were friends from childhood, routinely exchanged laps and did extra runs to help each other out. But even when riders did not know one another, had in fact never met before, they still volunteered to do extra laps when some mishap or illness or even just fear of what lay ahead on the trail prevented another rider from completing his lap.

This sense of brotherhood extended to the station managers and stock hands. If there was no one else to take on the lap, they would offer their help—choosing the smallest and lightest among them for the job. Horses were also part of this close-knit brotherhood. So much depended on them.

Many of the original Pony Express horses and almost all of those purchased as replacements for sick or injured horses were wiry little mustangs. Mustangs were descendants of the first horses the Spaniards had brought to the continent. Some of them had escaped into the wilderness, where they multiplied. Herds of them were now running wild, where they could be captured or, more easily, purchased from ranches in the area.

The training of mustangs was often quick and brutal. It consisted mainly of hurling the mustang to the ground when it refused to cooperate. It was considered trained as soon as it started to accept the added burden put upon its back. Most of the riders preferred these half-trained,

Wild mustangs frolic on the prairie in this painting by George Catlin, an American artist who travelled to the West to paint the Plains Indians in the mid-1800s. *(Smithsonian Museum of American Art)*

still-half-wild mustangs just the way they were. A few riders, like James Beatley, liked horses so wild that they would buck every time a rider approached it, saddle in hand.

One famous Pony Express story told of a big gray horse, probably of mixed breed, who so enjoyed racing through his lap that one day the urge to be off and running became too much for him. As soon as the mochila was taken from the back of the incoming horse and placed on his, the horse dashed off in a cloud of dust without waiting for the rider to mount, heading for the next station on his lap.

The deserted rider was given another horse to catch the runaway, but the substitute horse wasn't able to overtake the escapee. When the rider finally reached the station, he found the horse already there, patiently waiting to have the mochila taken from his back. The delighted men nicknamed the horse American Boy in reward for showing off its very independent spirit.

Sometimes it was the pluck and endurance of the horse that brought its rider through to safety. A handsome all-black mustang nicknamed Black Billy never failed to carry rider and mail through on his run, no matter what it might cost him. One day Black Billy arrived at the next station no longer a shining black mustang. The shocked station manager saw instead a horse covered in a mantle of blood and dust mingled together in a foamy rose lather. Two arrows protruded from Black Billy's body, one lodged in his shoulder, the other in his flank. Despite his injuries, the little mustang had brought his rider and the mochila through unharmed.

Natural causes, as well as the activities of hostile Paiutes, led to the loss of many horses. Urged to give their best during periods of extreme heat or extreme cold, a horse might drop dead of a heart attack mid stride. Occasional potholes were another hazard to the horse. Stumbling into one of these while going at a fast pace might break one or more of its legs. Unable to continue, it would have to be put down or left behind to be rescued by stockmen later.

George Edwin Little, not yet sixteen years old, was on a run from Salt Lake City to Rocky Ridge when he

A letter sent from New York to San Francisco via Pony Express in October 1860.

was overtaken by a heavy snowstorm. His horse, sloughing through deep drifts in bitter cold, suddenly dropped dead beneath him. Little managed to cut open the mochila, take out the mail, and cram it between his flannel shirt and his bare skin to keep it from contact with the snow. Then trudging through the drifts on foot, he carried the mail to Salt Lake City.

Often the bond between horse and rider was so close that a rider would put his life at risk in an effort to save his horse. Elijah Nickolas (Nick) Wilson was one of these riders. On his way to Shell Creek station he stopped at Spring Valley one noon to enjoy dinner with two young men there. Turning his horse loose to graze with the other horses in the meadow behind the station, he started to enjoy the meal until, glancing out of the window, he saw some Paiutes driving off all the horses, his own included.

Wilson and the other men were too late to stop the rustlers. But Wilson, not wanting to lose his horse, gave chase. Firing his pistol to drive off the Paiutes, he began threading his way through a grove of cedars. He hadn't gone far before a carefully aimed arrow tipped with a flint point whizzed from behind a cedar trunk to bury itself in Wilson's forehead two inches above his eye.

Wilson fell unconscious at the foot of the tree. When his companions found him, they tried to remove the arrow but failed. Finally, certain he was dead, they left him. Returning several days later to bury his corpse, they found him still clinging to life. They carried him back to the station house and summoned a doctor, who removed the flint but said there was nothing more he could do. For twelve days, Wilson hovered between life and death. Then he started to re-

After being shot in the forehead with an arrow, Nick Wilson always wore a hat to hide his scar.

cover. But until his death he bore the ugly scar left by the flint, the symbol of his devotion to his lost horse.

Melville Boughton had a better outcome when he attempted to rescue his horse. Arriving at the station at Thirty-two Mile Creek on his way to Fort Kearny, he discovered that thieves had just stolen his favorite mount. Station hands had already prepared a substitute for him and placed the mochila on its back. Boughton leapt upon the horse, but instead of heading for the next station he rode off after the thieves. He found them, chased them off with his rifle, and rescued his horse. He removed the mochila from the spare horse and, leaving it to find its own way back, he rode on to the next station, reaching it hours late but without an apology. On this occasion a rider had put his horse above the mail.

CHAPTER SEVEN

Trouble on the Trail

The warning Major Egan had passed along to his son had not been an empty one. As the month of April progressed, the Pony Express riders reaching Carson City were being deluged with cautionary tales about the potential for violence between white settlers and the native residents of the land.

Tension between the Paiutes and the whites was not a new problem. The conflict had begun back in the gold rush years, in the middle of the nineteenth century. The gold rush had lured thousands of people to California. Many of them had crossed Nevada to get there. Those that went by the southern route first followed the Humbolt River, then traveled across the desert to the Carson Sink, and over the Sierra Nevada, skirting Lake Tahoe.

Others had followed the northern route that led through

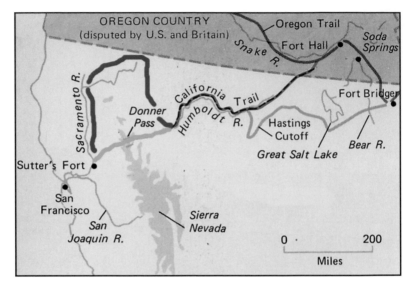

Gold seekers primarily took one of two routes to California, splitting off the California Trail along the Humboldt River. The northern route is marked in blue. The southern route, which involved crossing the infamous Donner Pass, is marked in green.

Virginia City, at the time a mining settlement because large quantities of silver and gold had been discovered nearby. This trail followed the Truckee River and passed through pleasant oases along the way. The oases followed the valley of the Truckee River and several lakes there, the largest being Honey Lake and Pyramid Lake.

The Paiutes and other tribes living there depended on the oases for their food—piñon nuts, edible grass seeds and tubers, and the wild animals that came to drink and feed there. It was these very places that also appealed to the newcomers. Many were farmers that had pulled up roots in the East and had now decided to stay here instead of going on to California. They began carving

The mining community of Virginia City boomed during the California gold rush.
(Library of Congress)

out small farms or ranches using the animals they had driven from the East as seed cattle.

As early as 1850, the number of settlers had increased to the point where they were starting to clash with the native peoples, whom they were crowding out of the choicest spots. What made things really difficult was that there seemed to be no common ground where two such different cultures could meet. The Paiutes and other native tribes who had lived there for centuries looked on the land as their sacred heritage. They depended on the great Earth Mother for life itself, and believed that, upon their death, she would gather them lovingly into her warm arms. To the whites, the land was

A Paiute woman grinds nuts or grain to prepare the daily meal. *(The Huntington Library, San Marino, California)*

just something to be used. Water, fertile soil, and good weather were all waiting to help bring crops to fruition. This meant that the land should be used to its fullest extent. Otherwise it was simply being wasted. And the Paiutes, who in the eyes of most of the whites were an ignorant, primitive people, were doing just that, and therefore should have no legitimate right to the best land.

Though it seemed useless even to try to reconcile these two opposite points of view, Old Chief Winnemucca,

Paiute leader Chief Winnemucca.

the principal Paiute chief at Honey Lake, tried his best to do so. He realized that the newcomers were not only there to stay but also would keep increasing their numbers. The best solution was to find some kind of agreement that would allow both sides to live together peaceably. In 1858, Chief Winnemucca had signed a treaty with the white settlers, each side promising to punish any member of its own group who was guilty of a violent act. To prove his sincerity, Chief Winnemucca had helped the settlers drive out the Pit peoples who were raiding the whites' potato gardens.

Chief Winnemucca's attitude changed when, in January of 1860, a settler was killed and the whites immediately accused him of harboring the murderer. The chief denied the charges, but the whites refused to believe him. They called in soldiers to search for the offender among Winnemucca's people. When the soldiers arrived to carry out the investigation, Winnemucca was furious. Though both sides had signed the treaty as equals, he realized he was being treated not as an equal but as an inferior person not worthy of respect. Otherwise the whites would never have called in the soldiers; they would have discussed the matter with him privately.

The chief would not tolerate such behavior. He immediately gave notice he was breaking the treaty and followed this with a demand of his own—$16,000 for the Honey Lake Valley that he claimed had been stolen from his people by the settlers. Winnemucca then sent out a summons to Paiute chiefs in the whole territory of Nevada. A Great Council was to be held at the tribal meeting place on the outskirts of Pyramid Lake. Its purpose was to discuss the growing problems with the white invaders.

The message was carried by runners who were received with enthusiasm everywhere but nowhere more so than along the Carson Sink. The winter of 1859-60 had been a season of terrible drought. Food had become so scarce that the local Paiutes were starving. Many of their children were dying, yet they did not dare accept the food the citizens of Carson City were offering them because they were convinced the whites were trying to poison them.

Soon chiefs from all over Nevada began gathering at the meeting place—old chiefs and young ones, high-ranking chiefs and minor ones. All were to be given an equal voice at the council. Chief Winnemucca was the most prominent chief there. Privately, he was in favor of war but he assumed an outward air of strict neutrality, saying only that he would agree with any decision made by the majority.

The meeting began with an open debate during which the Paiutes voiced their various grievances against the whites. There were many, and as the chiefs described them, their voices grew louder and angrier. They complained about the harvests of nuts lost to their people because the whites had chopped down the piñon trees just to start fires. They discussed the loss of game animals, from deer to desert hare and edible birds that once had contributed to the Paiutes' food supplies. They riled against the foreigners' guns that were so deadly the game had all been hunted out. And they talked about the destruction of the land itself, torn up by plows and then planted to foreign crops, destroying the native seed grasses and tubers on which the Paiutes depended.

Some chiefs complained about the singing wires that, strung on poles, had been spreading rapidly from the West Coast until they crossed the Sierra Nevada to come to rest at Carson City. What was the purpose of those wires? Was it to destroy the land entirely? The chiefs wanted to know.

Pony Express stations, although relatively unobtrusive, were still sites of unwanted activity for the Native Americans who lived nearby. *(Scotts Bluff National Monument)*

Then there were the Pony Express stations—though criticisms of them were milder. They did not take over large stretches of land, just enough for their modest buildings and a place to keep their horses. Since most of their food came from elsewhere, they had no need to torture the land as other whites did. And they readily shared their food with Paiute visitors.

As for the young men racing across the ancestral lands, the Paiutes had no real grudge against them either. The only things that disturbed them were the strange leather bags the young men carried. What the Paiutes really wanted was just to get hold of one of those bags and examine its contents.

So went the Great Council of chiefs when, one afternoon in early May, three drifters crossed over the Sierra Nevada following the trail that led to Carson City. Their names were Samuel Sullivan, James Fleming, and Dutch Phil, and they were probably fugitives from the law in California. The three bypassed Carson City and eventually showed up at Williams station, just east of the Carson Sink. Those three strangers, drunk and disorderly, had the power to set the flames of war sweeping across Nevada and western Utah, drawing in Pony Express riders and station people alike.

Williams station was named after its manager, J. O. Williams. At the time, Williams was away on a business trip, leaving his two younger brothers, David and Oscar, who were stock tenders, temporarily in charge. The younger men were green and easily bored by the humdrum life they were leading. One can imagine how they must have greeted the drifters when they arrived at the station, joking, laughing, and waving a whiskey bottle around. The brothers offered their new guests all the hospitality at their disposal—free room and an ample supper that night. The guests, in return, would have responded with frequent toasts to their generous hosts from the whiskey bottle they had brought with them.

With such a welcome, the drifters were certainly in no hurry to move on. They had apparently brought plenty of whiskey with them. They spent their time drinking and sleeping and, leaving the brothers to take care of their chores, wandering around in search of some excitement. Within a day or two they were going beyond

Although conceptions of the West and lawlessness became almost synonymous in the nineteenth century, the antics of the drifters at Williams station were actually rare. In most cases, the offenders would apologize and offer to pay for damages once they had sobered up. *(Amon Carter Museum, Fort Worth, Texas)*

the station grounds to case the surrounding countryside. There they came upon a company of Paiute women foraging. The women, used to the orderly behavior of the Williams men who had never bothered them, paid little attention to the newcomers who strolled around them, talking with one another in their strange tongue.

Suddenly, the men pounced on two of the women and dragged them off kicking and screaming, while the rest fled in terror. They took the women to a nearby canyon where they had found a cave. They barricaded the women inside.

Meanwhile, the other Paiute women raced to the husband of one of the captives, a minor chief. They told him that three white men staying at the Williams station had stolen his wife. The chief rode off to confront the Williams brothers, demanding that his wife be released at once. At this point the disaster could have been averted if the Williams brothers had confronted the drifters and ordered them to release the captives to the chief, and then placated the angry man with a lavish gift of food and an apology.

Instead, the Williams brothers let the drifters take over, perhaps by now afraid of opposing them because all three were armed. The drifters shook their guns at the chief and drove him out of the station. As he rode away, their taunts followed him. The chief did not respond. He had his own mission to accomplish. He sought out a chief named Mogoannoga who hated the whites and was looking for a good excuse to attack them. Mogoannoga listened to the grievances the other chief recited to him and became excited. Immediately, he sent out a call for his warriors to join him, and soon thirty followers had gathered.

The company of warriors set out for the Williams

station. They arrived midmorning to find the Williams brothers outside. Before the brothers could make a move or utter a sound, several of the Paiute warriors struck them down, killing them. Then, catching a glimpse of the drifter named Sullivan, who was attempting to slip away, they clubbed him down too.

Next they crashed through the station door to find the other two drifters lolling on their cots. When the men looked up to see the angry Paiutes storming into the room, they scrambled for their guns. Before they could reach them, they were killed. The Paiutes then sliced off the scalps of all five men and fastened them to the heads of their spears as trophies.

His honor avenged, the wronged Paiute chief found the cave and freed the captive women. Meanwhile, the other Paiutes cleared out all the provisions stored in the station house and then set fire to it. As it burned they danced around it in triumph. It was the first station house the Paiutes had destroyed, and it had fallen into their hands as easily as a ripe fruit. Whoever said the whites were invincible? They were weaklings!

The Paiutes went to work, dividing the provisions into various loads. They released the horses in the corral and some cattle from a nearby ranch. Shouldering their loads and driving the cattle and horses before them, they set off for Pyramid Lake and the Great Council of chiefs to proclaim their victory. But the provisions weighed them down, and the horses and cattle moved too slowly to satisfy them. Eager to brag of their victory, they sent a herald ahead to trumpet the exciting news: they had fought the whites and won easily.

On May 8, the older Williams returned to find his two brothers and the three drifters all dead and scalped. The station house was a smoldering ruin. The horses were gone, and the cattle from the adjacent ranch were missing. It was only much later that the story of the Paiute women's kidnapping that had started everything came to light. For the moment, Williams could not allow grief for his brothers to slow him down. If this was the beginning of a general uprising, the settlers and the Pony Express stations and riders would all be in peril. They had to be warned.

Without stopping to bury his brothers, Williams turned his horse around and galloped north to Virginia City. Close to the Paiute's council ground, it was also an area with many white settlements. If a war was to start, it would probably begin there. It was the point of greatest danger. All along the way, Williams sounded the alarm and asked others to help him spread it throughout Nevada.

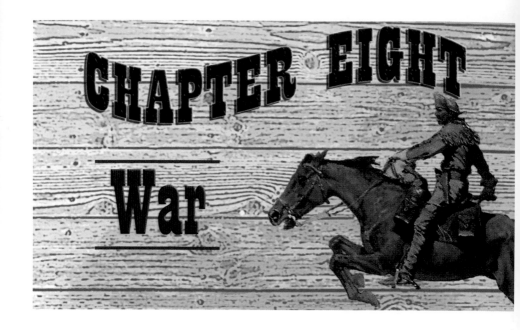

CHAPTER EIGHT
War

At the Great Council meeting, events were reaching a climax. The older chiefs were speaking in measured tones, but the younger ones were becoming more inflamed. Some had even begun clamoring for war. Numaga, also known as Young Winnemucca, was among the few younger chiefs who held back. He had had closer contact with the strangers than most and realized how much stronger they were than they appeared. Would there presently be more of them than the 8,000 or so Paiutes who had made this land their home? While there was still time, Numaga wanted to try to talk with the whites and strike some reasonable compromise that would avert war. But his voice was drowned in the general clamor.

Finally, Numaga left the council. He sought out a

Many of the western wars between Native Americans and settlers began as a result of settlers spreading throughout the West, and Native Americans being forced to relocate to find adequate food. *(Amon Carter Museum, Fort Worth, Texas)*

secluded spot. There he dropped to the ground hoping to draw strength, courage, and wisdom from the great Earth Mother. He lay there three days and nights, fasting and praying for his people. Fervently, he begged for guidance in speaking the right words that would sway his fellow chiefs. After his three-day fast, Numaga rose and returned to the council grounds. Relying on the great Earth Mother to give him the proper words, he began making a passionate appeal for peace.

Numaga's urgency silenced the clamor as the chiefs, drawn by the intensity in his voice, began listening to what he had to say. But in the midst of his speech, the

Paiute warrior and peacemaker Numaga. *(Nevada State Historical Society)*

herald sent by chief Mogoannoga arrived from Williams station. He burst into the council waving his spear triumphantly. He bragged about how easy it had been to overcome the weakling whites despite their guns. The chiefs sprang to their feet. The chance for peace had passed.

Meanwhile, the news of the slaughter at Williams station and the reports coming out of the Great Council were stirring up settlers everywhere. Eager to form a volunteer army and put the Paiutes in their place, settlers began gathering at various towns—Carson City, Gold Hill, Genoa, and Buckland's. When they learned that the volunteer army headquarters was being established at Buckland's, they all flocked there.

More than a hundred had soon gathered, many on horseback and all bringing their rifles, pistols, and plenty of ammunition with them. There were even a few soldiers among the volunteers. One of them was Bartholomew Riley, formerly a soldier stationed at Fort Lloyd. He had just been honorably discharged from the army and was on his way to join his family in California when he decided to help out the volunteers before moving on.

Another military man who showed up at Buckland's was Major William O. Ormsby, now retired. He immediately took charge of the volunteer army. First, he ordered them to bury the dead at Williams Creek. That done, he divided the volunteers into small military units. Once organized, they were off, going due north.

This painting by Frederic Remington shows the U.S. Cavalry on patrol on the western plains. In 1860, the army's forces in the West totalled about 10,000 men to cover 2.5 million square miles. These isolated, poorly equipped, and disorganized soldiers were sent to survey new routes and defend settlers, ranchers, and miners from potentially hostile western Indian tribes. *(Metropolitan Museum of Art, New York)*

By the eleventh day of May, they reached the Truckee River, where they came upon five worn-out stragglers who told them that for the last several days they had been fighting off attacks by Paiutes, who had already killed three of their friends. Relieved at the sight of so many recruits ready to take on the Paiutes, they promptly joined the makeshift militia.

As they progressed along the trail beside the Truckee River, the company lost all semblance of order. The neat units into which Ormsby had divided them soon became blurred and then disappeared altogether. The volunteers did not expect much from the Paiutes, certainly nothing resembling a real war. As far as they knew, the Paiutes were more accomplished as thieves, stealing potatoes from farmers' fields and driving off untended horses and cattle whenever they had a chance.

Meanwhile, the weather, though pleasant, was already verging on summer. Flowers brought up by the recent rains were still blooming and birds big and small were chattering in the underbrush. The event seemed more like an outing, or a casual picnic, than anything else. The volunteers, holding their rifles loose at their sides, strolled rather than marched along, laughing and joking among themselves. Even the horses kept to a lazy amble.

By May 12, they were following the ridge of a deep gorge through which, some fifty feet below them, the Truckee River rushed on its way to Pyramid Lake. As they neared the southern bank of the lake, sharp-ridged mountains began closing in from the east. The trail dropped sharply into the gorge. The settlers followed it to the narrow river valley floor, covered with a thick carpet of tall sagebrush.

Beyond the sagebrush stood a grove of cottonwood trees.

Except for the sound of the horses' hooves and the tramping boots of those afoot, everything was hushed, with no sign of an enemy anywhere. It was not until the advance company had passed through the cotton-wood trees that some two dozen warriors at last appeared, standing on a low rise of ground facing them, bows at the ready. Suddenly, the air was filled with flying arrows, their tips smeared with a deadly poison. For the first time the lighthearted crowd of volunteers realized they had walked into a trap. What they did not yet know was the extent of that trap. Around a bend in the river, hidden from view, were the clustered huts of the Paiutes' war camp.

The volunteers, realizing the danger of their exposed position, began retreating into the welcoming shelter of the cottonwood grove that had been so quiet and friendly when they had passed it. Now, they found it swarming with warriors armed with bows and arrows. The air resounded with the Paiutes' war whoops as they sprang out from behind the cottonwood trees. Horses reared, threw their riders, or were shot by the deadly arrows and dropped lifeless to the ground.

The panic-stricken volunteers lost all thought of discipline. In their haste to get out of the cottonwood grove, they trampled one another, or were trampled by the terrified horses. Major Ormsby tried to bring order to his demoralized army, but few listened to him, and his voice was soon stilled by a poisoned arrow that struck him in the mouth. Other arrows brought down his horse. As the triumphant Paiutes closed in on him, the major offered them his revolver, as was the custom in Europe when an army general surrendered to his enemy. But the Paiutes took his gesture as a sign of cowardice. In their culture no true warrior would have given in so meekly. He would have kept fighting to the end. They killed the major and took his scalp as their trophy.

Former lieutenant Riley now tried to take over the command. He fired shot after shot at the warriors that surrounded him. But try as he might, he could not rally the disorganized mob of volunteers that continued to rush for the open spread of sagebrush beyond the trees.

Another man just as brave as Riley tried to put an end to the bloodshed. He was young chief Numaga, who had attempted to quiet the cries for war at the council meeting. He stepped between the warriors and the stampeding volunteers and begged for a truce. But the Paiutes ignored him and rushed on after their quarry.

Some volunteers managed to break through the cottonwood grove into the open sagebrush that had seemed so empty before. To their shock they found it teeming with Paiute warriors. Leaping from the brush in which they had been so cleverly concealed, they sprang upon the fleeing men. Even after a few of the

Buckland's Pony Express station in the 1860s.

terrified volunteers reached the trail that led out of the trap and climbed it to the ridge above, they were still pursued by the Paiutes. The carnage stopped only when the Paiutes turned back, eager to get their share of the discarded loot—the rifles, pistols, ammunition, and horses left by the fleeing army.

On the ridge above, small groups of bewildered volunteers wandered about aimlessly. Bartholomew Riley took charge of the fifteen or so who gathered around him. He managed to lead them safely back to Buckland's, only to find the station people as shaken as his terrified charges. The Pony Express rider who was supposed to carry the waiting mochila on to Smith's Creek station, east of Buckland's, was refusing to go for fear of meeting the same fate as the Williams brothers.

Leaving his charges with the station manager, Riley

picked up the mochila, asked for a horse, and set off for Smith's Creek station. There he delivered the mochila to another waiting rider.

CHAPTER NINE
Stories and Legends

The day after J. O. Williams had discovered the remains of his brothers, Pony Express rider Bob Haslam set out from Friday station at the foot of Lake Tahoe on his customary run eastward. His lap would take him to Buckland's station, where he expected to hand the mochila over to the next rider, William Richardson. He arrived at Carson to find the town buzzing about the Williams station massacre. Rumors were floating everywhere, including that the Paiutes had launched an attack on settlers in the Honey Lake region and that they had killed two white men on the Truckee River.

As Haslam passed Hotel Penrock, he saw a number of men swarming around it. They were hauling in loads of rock to fortify the hotel. Many others had gone off to join the volunteer army that was gathering at Buckland's. So

"Pony Bob" Haslam in his later years.

many had left, commandeering all the horses in town, that Haslam couldn't find one to exchange for his own. He managed to get feed and water for his horse. After giving it a brief rest, he hurried on. Seventy-five miles beyond Carson City, he reached Buckland's station. By this time the volunteer army had already left under the command of Major William Ormsby. The only ones remaining at the station were W. C. Marley, the manager, and Richardson, who was to take the mochila from Haslam and carry it east. Haslam found both men in a panic. The news of the killings at Williams station had hit them hard. Richardson was so terrified that nothing could persuade him to take the mochila on. Marley turned to Haslam for help. Would he do the Richardson lap for a bonus of fifty dollars?

Haslam accepted the offer but not for the money, he explained. It was his obligation to see that the mail got through and, more importantly, to alert all the stations between Buckland's and Salt Lake City to the potential danger.

Placing the mochila on a fresh horse, Haslam was off again. Through Dry Creek, Sand Creek, and Cold Springs stations he rode carrying his message along with the mochila. To his relief he found all was quiet. At Smith's Creek he reached the end of Richardson's lap and found Jay G. Kelley waiting to carry the mochila and the ominous message eastward.

Haslam remained at Smith's Creek. He had ridden some 190 miles with scarcely a break and had earned a much-needed rest. Eight hours later, he was on his way back with the mochila Kelley had passed on to him.

Perhaps it was that eight-hour delay that saved Haslam's life. When he reached Cold Springs, he found the station house a blackened ruin, still smoldering. The body of the station manager, who such a short while before had given him a warm welcome, now lay sprawled in a pool of his own blood. The corral was empty—it was impossible to change horses here.

Haslam stayed only long enough to water and feed his horse from the store of hay untouched by the fire. Then he was off again. He found Sand Springs unharmed but deserted except for the stock tender. The others had all gone, he explained, but as long as there were horses to care for he couldn't leave. Haslam had a hard time

The ruins of Cold Springs station, made famous by "Pony Bob" Haslam's heroic ride. *(Nevada State Historical Society)*

persuading the man to go with him, but in the end he agreed, and the two set off together.

An overjoyed Marley greeted Haslam when he arrived at Buckland's Station. The manager had already given up Haslam for dead. He was so relieved at seeing the rider still alive that he raised his bonus to one hundred dollars.

At Buckland's, Haslam learned of the disaster that had befallen the volunteer army that left with such light hearts so short a time before. The fifteen terrified fugitives who remained told their story of ambush, rout, and massacre. And now, they said, there was no safety anywhere because Paiutes bent on destruction were roaming the whole region.

Haslam spent an hour and a half at Buckland's and then, despite the warnings of a concerned Marley, he rode on to Carson City. He found its people in deep mourning because many of the slain volunteers had come from this locality. Along with their grief there was a growing panic that the Paiutes might descend on the town itself. Women and children were being herded into the fortified Penrock hotel. Every man and many women were carrying loaded guns.

Carson City, Nevada, in 1860. *(Library of Congress)*

Haslam spent an hour and a half in Carson City. He had already ridden 380 miles and had been thirty-six hours on horseback, meeting dangers and obstacles all along the way. When he finally arrived at Friday station, where he had begun his perilous journey, he was just a few hours past his scheduled arrival time.

The story of Bob Haslam's epic ride was told everywhere and earned him the moniker "Pony Bob." As Pony Bob, he became another of the legendary tales that still surround the Pony Express.

The mourning and fear that had enveloped the settlements of Nevada quickly changed to anger and a determination to even the score. Thirty-six hours after the humiliating defeat of the volunteer army, word spread that a new army was gathering at Virginia City. Volunteers began arriving. Many came from California— from Sacramento and the gold towns of Downieville, Placerville, San Juan, and Nevada City. Other cities like San Francisco sent money in place of volunteers— money that was sorely needed to replace the guns and horses lost in the first battle and to provision the new expedition that was being organized. The largest number of volunteers came from Carson City, which had sustained the greatest losses.

On May 26, the volunteer army set out from Virginia City. Led by a military man, Colonel John C. Hayes, there were eight hundred men in all. Two hundred of them were soldiers supplied by various army forts scattered throughout the territory. Before leaving, Colonel

Hayes gave his motley army a solemn promise: whatever the outcome, he would excuse them after ten days
of service.

Better organized this time, and more sober, the volunteers hurried along the trail the first expedition had
followed. At the place where the trail dipped down into
the Truckee River valley, they came upon the twenty
bodies of their former comrades cut down by the pur-
suing Paiutes. The new volunteer army made camp at this
spot. While they buried their dead, Colonel Hayes sent
a small reconnaissance party down the trail into the
sagebrush expanse. They saw no one there, though they
kept a wary eye out for an ambush. Continuing on
through the cottonwood trees, they reached the open
meadow beyond—Bay Meadow, as they called it. Here
they found the bodies of twenty-six more men from the
first volunteer army.

It was in Bay Meadow that they finally sighted their
enemy. An array of Paiute warriors was waiting for them
on the same ridge from which they had greeted the first
army. Once again, as the enemy came into their sights,
the Paiutes began shouting at the whites below, shak-
ing their spears or the guns they had taken during the
previous battle. But they made no move to attack,
letting the reconnoitering party retreat to report their
findings to the rest of the army still waiting on the
upper trail.

Upon receiving the report, Colonel Hayes ordered his
troops down the trail. On June 3, the two armies met in

battle at Bay Meadow. To their shock, the Paiutes discovered that this was not the same kind of army they had attacked so successfully the first time. These were disciplined men determined to get their revenge. They had been forewarned of the possibility of an ambush so they were not surprised by the host of warriors that came running and shouting out of the cottonwood trees.

The two sides fought bravely, each holding its own. But after three hours of fierce combat, the Paiutes were forced to retreat into the mountains, leaving behind the bodies of twenty-six warriors and fifty horses. The victorious settlers went in pursuit of the Paiutes, but could not overtake them. Though the men spent the whole day searching, they could not find so much as a trace of their enemy. When dusk came, they gave up and made camp at Bay Meadow. The next morning, under orders from Colonel Hayes, they spent the day burying their dead and raising a crude fortification of mud and rock, which they called Fort Haven.

On the following day, leaving Captain Stewart and a few soldiers behind to guard the new fort, Colonel Hayes ordered his men back to Carson City. As soon as they arrived he dismissed them as he had promised. Only Captain Stewart and his men stayed at Fort Haven, keeping a watchful vigil until mid-July. When they did not see a single Paiute the whole time, they deserted the crude little fort and retraced their steps to Buckland's, where they built a proper fort, which they called Fort Churchill, and remained to man it.

The ruins of Fort Churchill, built in 1861 to defend settlers, and abandoned in 1870.
(Library of Congress)

The situation had now become a draw between the Paiutes and the settlers. But the Paiutes had learned something to their advantage. The Pony Express stations were as vulnerable as they appeared. The solitary riders could be brought down quickly. There seemed to be no strong protective magic in either the stations or the pouches. Emboldened by this realization, the Paiutes staged a wave of attacks on the stations. One by one they were destroyed—Cold Springs, Dry Creek, Simpson's Park, Reese River, and eastward through the poor huddles of stations in the desert, and on to the Ruby Mountain stations.

The station occupants either managed to flee in time or were killed, their corpses left beside the smoldering ruins and the broken-down corrals emptied of their horses. The solitary Pony Express riders were the most vulnerable. Many stories have been told of their exploits

In this painting by W. H. Jackson, a Pony Express rider gallops at breakneck speed, pistol ready, while being pursued during his delivery. *(Courtesy of Getty Images.)*

during this perilous time. There was the young Mexican rider shot by a hidden Paiute sniper as he galloped down the winding trail that led through Quaking Asp Grove to the nearby station. Mortally wounded, he managed to reach the station and deliver the mochila before he dropped dead.

The station manager had to find a substitute to carry the mochila on to the next station. He picked Jay G. Kelley. He was not only the lightest man there but he had also grown up around the Paiutes. Kelley took the mochila and set out at once. Coming to Quaking Asp Grove, he gave the horse its head and, holding his gun at the ready, set out on the winding narrow trail among the thronging aspen. He saw no one and caught no movement around him. Passing safely through the grove, Kelley reached the far side and open country again. But before he released his grip on the rifle to take up the reins, he gave a last sharp glance around him. His eye detected suspicious movements in a clump of shrubbery that hugged the fringe of the woods. With lightning precision he fired into it and the movements abruptly stopped. He took up the reins and was once again on his way.

It was only on Kelley's return ride that he saw how close he had come to death. On the same trail through Quaking Asp Grove, he came upon the bodies of six freshly killed soldiers, ambushed by the Paiutes. It was only Kelley's alertness that had saved him from the same fate.

Then there is the tale of fourteen-year-old Billy Tate. In 1980, a writer for *National Geographic* magazine, Rowe Findley, followed the Pony Express trail from St. Joseph, Missouri, to Sacramento, California, gathering anecdotes from old timers along the way

According to Findley's interviews, Billy Tate was one of the few orphans employed by the Pony Express. He was carrying a mochila from Ruby Valley to Salt Lake City. In the canyon country beyond Ruby Valley he found himself pursued by Paiutes. Setting spurs to his horse, Tate raced through the narrow rugged canyons with the Paiutes after him.

Finally, their arrows took down his horse. With no chance of outrunning the Paiutes and already badly wounded himself, Tate grabbed the mochila from the horse and took his stand behind a large boulder. With the boulder as his shield he faced his attackers, his gun at the ready. Billy Tate met them with shot after shot until he had emptied his gun. Then, his body peppered with arrows, he fell dead at their feet.

When Billy did not arrive at the next station, a search party was sent out to look for him. They found him lying where he had fallen. The bodies of seven Paiutes whom he had shot surrounded him. Beside him, untouched, lay the mochila the Paiutes had so coveted and which Billy had given his life to protect.

A simple statement written by one of the search party is quoted by Findley to explain why the Paiutes hadn't taken the mochila they so coveted. It reads in part: "They respected courage . . . They didn't touch the mochila."

The Paiutes hadn't scalped Billy either. In this way they had shown him the highest honor a Paiute could bestow on an enemy warrior.

CHAPTER TEN

Another Try

Bob Haslam's epic run was the last to leave from the West Coast. It was impossible to continue the Pony Express service under such perilous conditions. At the orders of Superintendent Bolivar Roberts in Sacramento and Major Egan in Salt Lake City, the Pony Express was temporarily discontinued until some kind of order could be established.

Meanwhile Frederick Dodge, the federal agent for Indian Affairs in Nevada, began laying out reservations for the Paiutes, including one around Pyramid Lake. At the same time, negotiations were opened between Numaga (Young Winnemucca) and the other more moderate chiefs to bring some semblance of order to the territory. As an added precaution, soldiers from various army posts began escorting the wagon trains of emi-

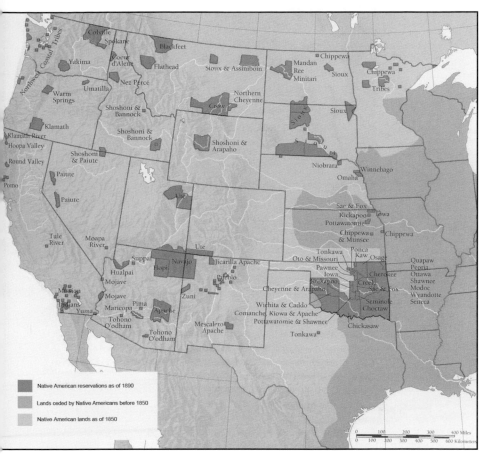

The diminishing lands of Native Americans in the nineteenth century.

grants who were still trying to pass through Nevada on their way to California. Platoons of soldiers started patrolling the whole area. But the Territory of Nevada was large and the numbers of soldiers available were few. Order was slow to return.

Nevertheless, by June 6, Major Egan felt it was safe enough to package the mochilas that had been stacking

THE PAIUTE

The Paiute were a migratory people who had lived in the western part of what is now the United States for thousands of years. They were divided into two branches: the Southern and the Northern, differing from each other in language and, to a lesser extent, in lifestyle. Both subsisted on the local game and vegetation, making them highly susceptible to problems caused by interference from outsiders.

The most famous of the Paiute was Wovoka, also known as Jack Wilson. In about 1870, he originated the Ghost Dance, a ritual that became central to a new religion combining elements of Christianity (from Wovoka's experience growing up in a white household) with Native American beliefs. Wovoka taught that whites would peacefully return the lands they had taken to their original inhabitants. Many of the Sioux killed by American soldiers at Wounded Knee (1890) were wearing ghost shirts, which they believed would keep them safe from bullets. Though Wovoka was an advocate of nonviolence, he lost much of his popular support after the massacre and faded into obscurity.

The Paiute were among those tribes moved onto reservations—lands the government set aside specifically for them but which were often ill-suited to the tribes' way of life or lacking sufficient natural resources for anything more than subsistence living. The Pyramid Lake reservation is still occupied by about 2,000 members of the Paiute, who have a government-to-government relationship with the United States and subsist mostly on revenues from fishing and other activities at the lake.

up in Salt Lake City and take them to Sacramento, and bring back those piling up there. He enlisted a volunteer army of his own to act as a convoy. Stacking the mochilas in wagons drawn by teams of mules, he set off westward.

At the same time, Bolivar Roberts started making plans to rebuild the ruined stations and get the express service started again. It wasn't going to be easy. The wars had cost the enterprise dearly. The company had seventeen employees slain by the Paiutes. Stations had been ransacked and some burned to the ground. Many of the company's horses had either been killed or stolen. He would need financial aid to start his project.

Roberts appealed to the city of Sacramento for donations. He said he would need $1,500 to pay the salaries of the people employed on the job. He had no trouble raising the funds. People in California had missed the services of the Pony Express and wanted it back again. Getting the guns and ammunition was no problem either. There were also plenty of workmen available because the people Roberts employed were mostly Pony Express riders and station employees temporarily out of work. Yet under the blistering heat of the desert summer, construction went forward slowly, partly because Roberts was replacing the flimsy old shacks with more substantial buildings.

As each station was completed it was stocked with provisions. Horses were brought in, and a station manager and stockmen arrived. Before Roberts went on to the next station, he left behind armed sentinels to guard the rebuilt station. By the first of July, Roberts had reached Roberts Creek, where he met with Major Egan moving westward.

This picture, entitled *Pursuit,* was published in the *Illustrated London News* in 1861. Although the artist is said to have witnessed the arrival and departure of Pony Express riders in St. Joseph, there are several noticeable discrepancies from other descriptions: the rider is too heavy; he would have carried a pistol instead of a rifle; and he is using a saddlebag mail pouch instead of the standard mochila. *(Library of Congress)*

Finally, on July 7, the Pony Express was ready to run again. But despite the added strength in the newly fortified stations and the presence of companies of dragoons patrolling the area, both the stations and Pony Express riders were still vulnerable. Though a kind of peace had finally been agreed upon between the two sides, there was no central Paiute authority to enforce it. Minor chiefs and their followers were still free to do as they pleased.

All through the summer and into the fall, small bands of rebellious warriors continued to harass stations and solitary riders. The largest of these attacks took place in October at the station house in Egan Canyon. It may have been spurred on by the approach of winter, a time of year when food would be scarce.

Egan Station had always been one of the most vulnerable in the chain of Pony Express stations. The narrow canyon in which it was situated was well suited to ambush. More than once, the Paiutes had set traps for the riders racing down the winding trail. Fortunately, the riders themselves had grown up in this area and had learned how to figure out most of the Paiutes' moves before they made them.

One morning in October, station manager Mike Holt and rider Nick Wilson were eating breakfast at Egan Station. Wilson was waiting for the mochila from the West to arrive so that he could exchange it for the one he carried and be on his way back east.

Suddenly the men were surprised by a loud commotion in the compound outside. Looking out of a window they saw a crowd of some eighty Paiute warriors who had just burst onto the premises. Both men snatched up their guns and prepared to do battle with the intruders. Standing in the open doorway they fought off the Paiutes until their ammunition ran out. Then the Paiutes burst into the station house. Over the babble of voices the chief's shout finally made itself heard. He was calling for bread.

Holt had recently baked a batch of it. He and Wilson now brought out the loaves and stacked them on the table, hoping it would satisfy their hungry guests and they would then leave.

The two men watched as the Paiutes stuffed great chunks of bread into their mouths and wolfed them down. Soon all the loaves were gone. But instead of leaving, the chief pointed at the sacks of flour stacked on the station house floor. Holt gestured to the chief, making it plain that they were all his for the taking. The chief shook his head vehemently. With the scant words he had at his disposal, along with meaningful gestures, he made it clear that he wanted all the sacks of flour converted into loaves too.

Holt obediently built a fire and heated the oven. He began turning the flour into dough, then filling his baking pans and putting them in the oven. As soon as one batch was turned out, the Paiutes grabbed the loaves. Hot as they were, they wolfed them down and demanded more. As the day wore on, bag after bag of flour was turned into loaves.

While they worked, Wilson and Holt worried about William Dennis, the rider for whom Wilson was waiting. At first they were afraid that, unaware of what was going on, he would burst in upon the warriors, who would kill him instantly. But the day wore on and Dennis still did not appear. The two men began to fear he had already been murdered along the way.

The sun was nearing the western horizon as the last of the flour was baked into loaves and devoured. Now, perhaps, the Paiutes would realize there was nothing more to be had here and would leave, allowing their captives free to go in search of Dennis. Instead, the chief uttered a few orders in his own tongue.

In response, several warriors seized Holt and Wilson

and dragged them outside. There they saw to their horror that the long wooden tongue of a station farm wagon had been planted in the earth creating an upright stake. The warriors pulled Holt and Wilson to the stake and tied them firmly to it with ropes they found in the station house. The rest of the warriors began gathering armloads of dried sagebrush, which they stacked around the men at the stake. When everything was ready the Paiutes set the brush afire.

Unnoticed by the warriors or their captives, a solitary figure appeared in the distance—William Dennis. He had met with no harm and was just late in arriving. From down the road he had heard unusual noises. Now he was approaching stealthily to see what was going on. Presently the whole scene became plain to him—the milling warriors, the crackling flames as the sagebrush caught on fire, and in the center two men tied to a stake. He could guess who they were.

Dennis whipped his horse around and began racing back the way he had come. He was heading for the company of soldiers he had just passed some five miles back. Once within earshot he shouted out his story. At the news the company broke into a gallop. Bugles blaring, they charged ahead. They burst upon the shocked warriors, scattering them. But after that first surprise, the Paiutes turned and fought fiercely while Dennis stamped out a pathway through the flames and released the bound men.

The fighting continued as twilight deepened into

dusk. The Paiutes retreated with the approach of night, disappearing into the darkness beyond the sputtering fire. They left behind the bodies of eighteen of their warriors and sixty horses. The soldiers themselves also had to pay a price. In the little graveyard above Egan Station lie the graves of twenty-five dragoons. At least some, if not all of them, fell on this October night.

Despite the sporadic raids of Paiutes on stations and riders, the Pony Express managed to continue its service. But a new challenge awaited it—winter weather in the Sierra Nevada. For almost fifteen years, the people in the area had been haunted by the dreadful fate that had befallen the Donner party—a pioneer group making its way to California late in the season of 1846. Caught in a blizzard at a place off the northern shore of Lake

This painting by eastern artist Albert Bierstadt, who came to the West in 1859 as part of a government survey, depicts the beautiful yet infamous Donner Pass in the Sierra Nevada. *(New York Historical Society)*

Tahoe that came to be called Donner's Pass, what followed was a horrible tale of suffering and death from cold and starvation. People driven by gnawing hunger even resorted to cannibalism to get what they could from the emaciated corpses of their dead comrades, until help finally arrived from the California lowlands.

Ever since then, the Sierra Nevada had been deemed impassable during the winter months. That was the reason John Butterfield of the Butterfield Overland Mail Company had turned away from the central route. There seemed to be no way a solitary Pony Express rider could make it through in the wintertime.

The Pony Express riders were ready to accept the challenge. The mail had to be transported to California as quickly as possible. Political updates were especially important since the Union was being threatened by the increasingly harsh rhetoric expressed by Northern and Southern House and Senate leaders in Washington, D.C.

Things were even more tense than usual in 1860 because of an approaching election. The future of the Union would rest on the shoulders of the man who would become president after the election in November. And Californians would help to elect that man. Before they voted, it was important for them to get all the information they could about the nominees. The chief competitors were the silver-tongued orator, Stephen Douglas, a favorite of the South, and his opponent, the awkward young lawyer from Illinois, Abraham Lincoln, nominee of the newly formed Republican Party. The two sparred with

THE ELECTION OF 1860

The election of 1860 was one of the most crucial presidential elections in the United States' history. The political, social, and economic differences between the North and the South had been growing since the Missouri Compromise of 1820. As more and more territories organized and petitioned to become states, the question of how—or whether—to maintain the balance between the number that permitted slavery and the number that did not became more urgent. The country was divided between proslavery, antislavery, and popular sovereignty camps. Popular sovereignty (the doctrine that residents of each state should be able to vote to decide whether to permit slavery in their state) proved problematic, leading to riots in Kansas and Nebraska in the 1850s.

A political divide reflected the popular divide. The Whig Party was dissolved when many Southerners left it to join the Democratic Party. The new Republican Party, formed in 1854, represented the antislavery stance and sent Abraham Lincoln to the polls in 1860. The Democrats of the North nominated Stephen Douglas, who retained a belief in the possibility of popular sovereignty to allow for peace, while those in the South sent John C. Breckinridge as their candidate. A fourth entrant, John Bell, stood for the Constitutional Union Party. Lincoln's strong opposition to the expansion of slavery led Southerners to threaten secession if he was elected. When he was, by a minority of the popular vote, the South revolted and the nation was soon at war.

each other in a series of debates that inflamed the country.

Along the Pony Express route, where Northerners and Southerners were almost equally represented, arguments frequently broke out between the two sides. The

Democratic presidential candidate Stephen Douglas.
(Library of Congress)

arguments usually resulted in no more than a switching of flags displayed by a shop, restaurant, or boarding house. More serious were the arguments that took place in cities where, heated by words, opposing sides began settling matters with guns. Things became so unruly in San Francisco that for a while vigilante groups took over maintaining order, their hasty verdicts carried out immediately by a waiting hangman.

When Election Day arrived, people across America flocked to the polls to cast their votes. It would be close, especially in California. By a narrow margin the vote in San Francisco went to Stephen Douglas. Statewide, with almost as narrow a margin, Lincoln won. The state now

A letter intended for a Denver newspaper bringing news of Lincoln's election via Pony Express. *(Denver Historical Society)*

waited in suspense for the outcome of the national vote.

At midnight November 6, an announcement was made at last. Abraham Lincoln had won the election. To get the news to the West Coast as quickly as possible, the fastest Pony Express riders were chosen. Relay after relay, they raced across the continent, arriving at Sacramento in eight days, two short of the ten-day delivery schedule.

In the East, events were moving swiftly. Lincoln's election was enough for South Carolina. The state had previously threatened to secede if he became president. On December 20, it did so. By February 1, 1861, six other states—Mississippi, Florida, Alabama, Georgia, Louisiana, and Texas—had joined South Carolina. The seceding states now formed their own republic, naming Jefferson Davis their president.

On March 4, 1861, Lincoln gave his inaugural speech.

President Abraham Lincoln. *(Library of Congress)*

It was hard hitting but also conciliatory. He would not immediately free slaves, he promised. The states that now allowed them could keep them. But on one point there could be no compromise. Secession of any state from the Union was unacceptable. "The union of these states is perpetual," he pointed out. "We are not enemies,

In this print, a Pony Express rider switches his horse and mochila at a relay station. The time allotted for such a transaction was approximately three minutes.

but friends. . . . Though passion may have strained, it must not break our bonds of affection."

The speech in its entirety was sent west by Pony Express. The fastest of the horses were chosen to carry it, along with the best riders. Joseph Barney Wintle was one of the riders. He carried the mochila from Fort Kearny to Cottonwood Springs, a distance of 110 miles. Wintle rode it without stopping to change horses at intervening stations along the way. He arrived at Cottonwood Springs in five hours' time, breaking a record. But his valiant horse, unable to bear the strain, dropped dead of a heart attack as the mochila was being lifted from its back.

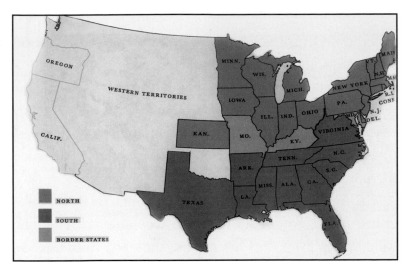

This map shows the breakdown of the states that supported slavery (the South) and the free states (the North) on the eve of the Civil War. While California and Oregon were admitted into the union as free states, their primary involvement in the war was the contribution of a nominal amount of troops.

There was no time to grieve over the fallen horse; the message had to continue on its way with all possible speed. Back in Washington, D.C., events were moving swiftly to a climax. Lincoln's speech had made little impression on the seceding states and certainly not on South Carolina. Major Robert Anderson, the Union officer in charge of Fort Sumter, which guarded South Carolina's principal port, Charleston, now found himself surrounded by hostile and determined Southerners. Their anger was soon expressed in action. On April 12, 1861, Confederate batteries began shelling Fort Sumter. Short of ammunition and with only a skeleton force at his disposal, Anderson had to surrender.

On April 19, Lincoln issued his proclamation of war. The proclamation drove four more states into the Confederacy—Virginia, Arkansas, Tennessee, and North Carolina. California had chosen to back the Union. As a Union state, she added an important contribution to the war effort. Shiploads of California gold and Nevada silver left San Francisco for Union ports on the East Coast. They were funds the Union desperately needed to replenish its fast-dwindling war chest.

California was also assigned a quota of 17,000 recruits, her share to help fight the secessionists. The men were drawn from forts around the state and from the San Francisco Presidio that guarded the bay. Other young men went as volunteers. Some joined the Union forces, others the Confederacy. Sometimes best friends joined opposite sides and fought against each other. So it went, friend against friend, even brother against brother or father against son, as the country plunged into a bloody and terrible war.

In the months that followed the surrender of Fort Sumter, the news carried westward by the Pony Express was not good. On July 12, the battle of Bull Run was fought at Manassas. It ended with the rout of the Union army, heralding the South's second victory. The only reason the rebel forces did not march straight into Washington, D.C., was the large number of casualties they had taken and the utter exhaustion of their troops.

When the news of the battle of Bull Run arrived in San Francisco, the city was swept by fear and uncertainty. The navies of Great Britain, Russia, and France were hovering just outside the bay as was their custom.

But now with the soldiers gone from the Presidio and the cannon in it antiquated and almost useless, San Franciscans felt exposed and vulnerable. The news brought to them twice weekly by the Pony Express was the only slender thread that connected them with their government thousands of miles away to the east, which was itself beleaguered by rebel forces.

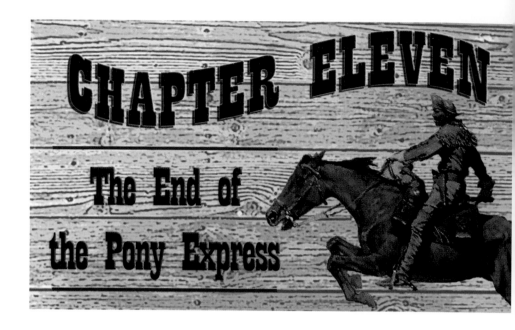

CHAPTER ELEVEN

The End of the Pony Express

The Pony Express riders had made it through a terrifying winter in the Sierra Nevada, exploding the myth that the mountains were impassable and deadly in wintertime. They had proved that seasoned riders used to winters in the mountains could handle whatever dangers they encountered to deliver important mail in record time. They had also proved invaluable in bringing closer contact between California's state capital at Sacramento and the national government in Washington, D.C., especially during the early chaotic months of the Civil War.

With its many successes the Pony Express had earned its place in history. Yet it was now facing one of the greatest threats of all. The firm of Russell, Majors & Waddell was on the verge of bankruptcy. It had embarked on the Pony Express venture at a time when the company was already in debt. Much of the debt was incurred because the United States government had been slow paying the some $600,000 it owed for valuable transportation services that had been provided to the Defense Department. Fully expecting the money to be paid, Russell had been able to convince his partners to launch the Pony Express venture. If it proved successful, as he was sure it would, the firm would get the government contract to carry mail on the central route and a subsidy to help defray expenses.

The Pony Express had proved itself with superb skill but it had also been an additional drain on the company's finances. One of the largest of these new expenditures was the $75,000 the Paiute wars had cost. Saddled with these mounting expenses, Russell finally went to Washington, D.C., to pressure the government for immediate payment of its debt. He was told that the appropriations granted the Defense Department for such services had run out. Russell, Majors & Waddell would have to wait for their money until Congress met and voted on the necessary funds.

Russell spent a lot of time in Washington trying to borrow money to pay the firm's most pressing debtors. Finally, in desperation he accepted the help of a friend in government who had access to the national Indian trust funds. The friend offered Russell the use of a number of these bonds to tide him over.

Against his better judgment, Russell accepted the offer. He used part of the bonds as collateral to borrow

THE BUREAU OF INDIAN AFFAIRS

Indian trust funds were set up and managed by the Bureau of Indian Affairs (BIA). The BIA was created in 1824. It had jurisdiction over the removal of Native Americans to the West and was charged with maintaining the peace and ensuring those populations were cared for. It failed miserably at most of these duties, including protecting the money owed to Native American tribes.

When land was sold or revenues were earned from grazing rights or other leases, that money was supposed to be held in trust. Allegations of misuse of those funds have been levied against the U.S. government for years, finally culminating in a 1996 lawsuit, *Cobell v. Norton*. Three years later, the court ruled the U.S. government had indeed breached its responsibility to the individuals and tribes it was supposed to care for. Since then, the government has been working to reform the current system and investigate past mismanagement. The extent of that mismanagement is difficult to calculate, partly because so many records have been lost or destroyed, but current estimates say Native American trusts have been cheated out of more than $2.4 billion dollars.

some of the money he needed. He got more by selling other bonds outright. In this way he was able to stave off the most urgent creditors. But Russell had a price to pay for taking the bonds. The shady business transaction was discovered and he was accused of fraud, jailed, and indicted by Congress—though he was later released and never brought to trial. He was, however, asked to leave the firm in 1861.

Though this event cast a cloud over the reputation of the firm, the potential promise of the Central mail route contract kept it in business until the outbreak of the Civil War. Up until then, the Butterfield Overland Mail Company, founded by several large companies, including Wells Fargo, had made a success of carrying passengers and mail to the West by the southern route. But news of gunfire at Fort Sumter followed by the declaration of war between the North and the South worked against the Overland Mail Company. The trail that had previously been so promising became dangerous, because for much of the way it ran through states that were committed to the Confederacy.

Since the Butterfield line was connected to Northern business interests, it had become the object of attacks by Southern sympathizers. There were frequent raids

A Wells Fargo wagon transports a shipment of gold from Deadwood, South Dakota. Four armed security guards ride along to deter robbers. *(Library of Congress)*

upon stagecoaches and any passengers who still dared to travel that way. Finally, the road itself became so torn up it was impassable. The line had no choice but to close its operations and move north to the central route now that the Pony Express riders had proved it passable in all seasons.

When the Overland Mail Company moved north, it began competing directly with the Russell, Majors & Waddell firm. Both applied for a government contract to carry the mail and a subsidy to help finance the operation. Despite the fine organizational skills Russell, Majors & Waddell had displayed, Congress passed it over and awarded the contract and the subsidy to the Overland Mail Company. This marked the beginning of the end of the great freighting firm known as the Central Overland California & Pike's Peak Express Company.

The massive debt the government owed the firm was never paid, though it did replenish the Indian trust funds with interest, sparing Russell that expense. But it was not enough to enable Russell, Majors & Waddell to recoup their losses.

One last challenge threatened the continued exist-ence of the Pony Express. It came from the growing telegraph service. In 1812, Samuel Morse had invented a method by which electricity could be used to carry messages over great distances. He had devised a code, known as the Morse Code, which was a kind of short-hand for such messages. Since then, the eastern and

OVERLAND MAIL ROUTE
TO CALIFORNIA.

Through in Six Days to Sacramento!

CONNECTING WITH THE DAILY STAGES

To all the Interior Mining Towns in Northern California and Southern Oregon.
Ticketed through from PORTLAND, by the

OREGON LINE OF STAGE COACHES!

And the Rail Road from Oroville to Sacramento,

Passing through Oregon City, Salem, Albany, Corvallis, Eugene City, Oakland,
Winchester, Roseburg, Canyonville, Jacksonville, and in California—
Yreka, Trinity Centre, Shasta, Red Bluff, Tehama, Chico,
Oroville, Marysville to SACRAMENTO.

TRAVELERS AVOID RISK of OCEAN TRAVEL

Pass through the HEART OF OREGON—the Valleys of Rogue River, Umpqua and Willamette.

This portion of the Pacific Slope embraces the most BEAUTIFUL and attractive, as well as some of the most
BOLD, GRAND and PICTUERESQUE SCENERY on the Continent. The highest snow-capped mountains, (Mt. HOOD,
Mt. SHASTA and others,) deepest ravines and most beautiful valleys.

Stages stop over one night at JACKSONVILLE and YREKA, for passengers to rest.
Passengers will be permitted to lay over at any point, and resume their
seats at pleasure, any time within one month.

FARE THROUGH, FIFTY DOLLARS.

Ticket Office at Arrigoni's Hotel, Portland.

H. W. CORBETT & Co.,

PORTLAND, July 19, 1866.

Proprietors Oregon Stage Line.

[W. B. Carter, Printer, Front St., Portland, Oregon.]

This advertisement, promoting the Overland Mail Company's service along the
more northern routes west, focuses on the convenience and scenic benefits of
such a trip and wisely avoids mention of the potential perils of the journey. *(The
Bancroft Library)*

Samuel Morse, inventor of the electric telegraph and originator of Morse Code. *(Library of Congress)*

western coasts of the United States had been putting the Morse Code to use by spinning a web of electrical wires across the settled parts of their regions.

Attempts were also being made to carry telegraphic service across the continent. To the west the telegraph line, after mounting and descending the Sierra Nevada, stopped at Carson City. To the east the cross-continent telegraph line stopped at Fort Kearny, east of the Rocky

One of Morse's telegraph keys. The message would be keyed out in Morse Code using this device, then transmitted over wire to the receiver, who would then translate the message into words.

Mountains. The wide gap between the two terminals contained some of the wildest landscapes in the continent—the massive Rocky Mountains, jumbles of ridges, narrow canyons, turbulent rivers, and desolate deserts.

For a while there had been no hurry to bridge this gap, because the Pony Express had solved the problem adequately. The riders just stopped to pick up any telegrams waiting at one terminal and then carried them to the terminal at the other end. The outbreak of the Civil War ended this complacency. Instant telegraph service between east and west suddenly became vital to the United States government. Crews were issued a mandate: military necessity required that both lines be connected as quickly as possible.

In an effort to inspire the two crews, a race was announced. Salt Lake City was named the midpoint. Whichever crew arrived there first would win all the monies brought in by the east and west telegraph services until the losing team also reached the meeting place. This got things off to a good start.

Intrigued by the promise of a race, people everywhere in the North began laying wagers on which crew would reach the goal first. Inspired by the glory of winning a national race, both sides broke into a whirl of activity. Teams of lumbermen rushed to the mountains to harvest trees with straight trunks that could be shaped into poles. Then the poles were loaded onto wagons and hauled by teams of oxen or mules to the work sites. Insulated wire, manufactured only on the East Coast, was brought to the eastern work site by slow moving oxen. To get to the western work site, the bails of wire traveled by sailing ship, circling Cape Horn and on to San Francisco. From there the wire was carried by mule train to its destination.

Despite all the obstacles, the poles went up, marching westward and eastward. The tribes who lived along the route of the singing wires viewed the activity with growing alarm. They began attacking the poles, chopping them down and scattering the dead wires everywhere. In some places violent skirmishes broke out between workers and warriors. At times the United States army had to send in troops to protect the project. Still the work on both sides went forward rapidly, much of it inspired by the wagers made on the crews.

The Pony Express riders also played their part in keeping alive the competitive spirit. Each rider, as he

Newly constructed telegraph poles stretch into the horizon as a Pony Express rider passes, noting the progress. The success of the telegraph would eventually render the Pony Express obsolete. *(Courtesy of the Granger Collection.)*

picked up and delivered telegrams, would pass along the latest news on the progress of the other side. Finally, on October 20, 1861, the crew from the East arrived in Salt Lake City to claim the prize. It was a slim prize at best because the crew from the West arrived on October 24, only four days later.

With the two ends of the telegraph service now joined, communication across the continent became instantaneous. The days of the Pony Express were almost over. The men who were still on their last laps would shortly complete the final runs. All the riders would then be disbanded to go on to more lucrative employment.

A short time later, overwhelmed with debt, the Central Overland California & Pike's Peak Express Company

NOTICE.

BY ORDERS FROM THE EAST,

THE PONY EXPRESS

WILL be DISCONTINUED.

The Last Pony coming this way left Atchinson, Kansas, yesterday.

oc25-1t **WELLS, FARGO & CO., Agents.**

This notice was published by the Wells Fargo Company in the San Francisco *Bulletin* on October 26, 1861. *(Bancroft Library)*

was forced to announce bankruptcy proceedings. Soon afterwards the three partners dissolved their partnership and went their separate ways.

The Pony Express left behind an emptiness that was felt all along the route over which the ponies had galloped. The hoof beats of a speeding horse would no longer be heard announcing the arrival of news, letters, and a breath of home so far away. Perhaps those most affected by the loss of the Pony Express were the Californians, who had come to depend so much on the young riders. Though the singing wires were making instant communication between east and west now possible, they could never touch the hearts as had the conscientious young men who had so often put their lives at risk to keep the pledge they had made: the mail must go through. A San Francisco paper of the time, *The Pacific,* printed a farewell to the riders. It read in part: "You came to us often with tidings that made your feet beautiful . . . We have looked for you as those who wait for the morning, and how seldom did you fail us! When days were months and hours were weeks, how you thrilled us out of our pain and suspense, to know the best or know the worst! You have served us well."

Afterword

Preserving the Pony Express Trail

Despite the achievements of the Pony Express, it was replaced by the development of technology—the success of the overland telegraph in October 1861, and then the completion of the continental rail service. Even during the period of its run, the Pony Express was overshadowed by the events of the Civil War and might have become just a footnote in history except for the efforts of Buffalo Bill Cody, himself a Pony Express rider in his youth. He rekindled interest in it by including Pony Express episodes in his Wild West shows, keeping alive the romance and history of the unique mail service.

A desire among history buffs and horsemen to recreate the Pony Express led to the first rerun of the mail service in 1923. Sixty volunteer riders followed the trail through eight states. Twelve years later in 1935, a second run of the Pony Express took place, this time to celebrate the Pony Express centennial, the hundredth anniversary of the Pony Express. Relays of horses and volunteer riders carried a mochila holding commemorative letters from St. Joseph to San Francisco. Later, the Centennial Commission marked the trail and the remount stations with bronze tablets.

This was the beginning of a contemporary interest in the Pony Express resulting in numerous books, movies, and commemorative events, along with efforts to preserve the trail as an important historical site. As early as 1966, an ongoing movement had begun to re-ride the trail. These events culminated in the formation of the National Pony Express Association (NPEA) in 1979.

Today some eight hundred members belong to the association. They not only come from almost every state in the Union but also from such foreign nations as Germany, England, and the Czech Republic, all stirred by the continuing romance of the Pony Express.

In 1980, interested members took part in a complete re-ride of the Pony Express trail, beginning in Sacramento, California, and ending in St. Joseph, Missouri. Since then, a commemorative re-ride of the trail is made each June between these two overland terminal cities, and mail is carried to a new generation. Aside from these reruns, the NPEA is active throughout the year working with community groups and visiting schools to talk to the pupils about American history and the part the Pony Express played in it. The NPEA also works with the

National Park Service, the United States Forest Service, and the Bureau of Land Management to preserve the trail, the trail sites, and their history. Other projects include clearing brush and timber, and bridging creeks on backcountry trails so that hikers and equestrians (and their horses) can travel safely.

On August 13, 1992, due to the efforts of the NPEA and other concerned organizations, the Pony Express Trail was finally added to the National Trails System as a National Historical Trail. By this time many states and local governments, as well as many community historical associations, were also doing their part to preserve the memory of the Pony Express. Former stations were converted into museums with exhibits portraying Pony Express history. During commemorative events the stations were returned to use. Here and there along the trail, monuments of the riders and their mounts stand, larger-than-life reminders of the young boys and the gallant horses that carried the Pony Express mail, and with it a vibrant part of Old West history.

Larry Carpenter
Corresponding Secretary
National Pony Express Association

List of Riders

ne of the Central Overland & Pike's Peak Express company records contain
authentic list of riders dating back to the days when it was in operation.
is list has been compiled from a variety of sources, but is not thought to
complete.

ck Alcott	Hugh Brown	Frank Derrick
hn Anson	James Brown	Alex Diffenbacher
nton	James Bucklin	Thomas Dobson
enry Avis	John Burnett	J. Dodge
odney Babbit	Ed Bush	Joseph Donovan
. W. Ball	William Campbell	Tom Donvan
afayette Ball	Alexander Carlyle	W. E. Dorrington
mes Banks	William Carr	Calvin Downs
mes Barnell	William Carrigan	Daniel Drumheller
m Baughn	James Carter	James E. Dunlap
lelville Baughn	William A. Cates	William Eckles
larve Beardsley	James Clark	Major Howard Egan
mes Beatley	John Clark	Howard Ransom Egan
harles Becker	Richard W. Clark	Richard Erastus Egan
homas Bedford	Richard Cleve	Thomas J. Elliot
harles Billman	Charles Cliff	J. K. Ellis
. R. Bills	Gustavas Cliff	Charles Enos
Black Sam"	William F. Cody	George Fair
Black Tom"	Buck Cole	H. J. Faust
homas Black	Bill Corbett	Josiah Faylor
afayette Bolwinkle	Edward Covington	Johnny Fischer
ond	James Cowan	John Fisher
Boston"	Jack Crawford	William F. Fisher
Villiam Boulton	James Cumbo	Thomas Flynn
hn Brandenburger	Louis Dean	Jimmie Foreman
harles H. ("Doc") Brink	William Dennis	Johnny Fry

Abram Fuller
George Gardner
James Gentry
James Gilson
Samuel Gilson
James Gleason
"Irish Tom" Grady
Frank Gould
Sam Hall
Samuel Hamilton
William Hamilton
George Harder
"Pony Bob" Haslam
Theodore Hawkins
Sam Haws
Frank Helvey
Levi Hensel
William Hickman
Chas. Higgenbotham
Martin Hogan
Clark Huntington
Lester Huntington
William James
David R. Jay
William D. Jenkins
Jennings
Samuel Jobe
William Jones
Jack Keetley
Hi Kelley
Jay G. Kelley
Mike Kelly
Thomas O. King

John P. Koerner
Harry La Mont
William Lawson
George Leonard
George E. Little
Elias Littleton
"Tough" Littleton
N. N. Lytle
Sye Macaulas
Robert Martin
Elijah Maxfield
Montgomery Maze
Emmet McCain
J. G. (Jay) McCall
Charlie McCarty
James McDonald
Pat McEarney
David McLaughlin
James McNaughton
William McNaughton
Lorenzo Meacona
J. P. Mellen
Howard Mifflen
Charlie (Bronco) Miller
James Moore
Jeramiah H. Murphy
Newton Myrick
Matthew Orr
Robert Orr
G. Packard
William Page
John Paul
"Mochila Joe" Paxton

George W. Perkins
William Prindham
Thomas J. Ranahan
Theodore (Yank) Rand
James Randall
Charles Reynolds
Thomas J. Reynolds
William Minor Richard
H. Richardson
Johnson W. Richardson
Bartholomew Riley
Jonathan Rinehart
Don C. Rising
Harry Roff
Edward Rush
Robert Sanders
G. G. Sangiovanni
George Scovell
John Seerbeck
Jack Selmen
Joseph Serish
John Sinclair
George Spurr
William H. Streeper
Robert Stricklen
William Strohm
John W. Suggett
Billy Tate
Josiah Taylor
George Thatcher
J. J. Thomas
Bill Thompson
Charles F. Thompson

"Cyclone" Thompson
James M. Thompson
Alexander Topence
W. S. Tough
George Towne
Henry Tuckett
Warren (Boston) Upson
W. E. van Blaricon

John B. Wade
Henry Wallace
Daniel Westcott
Michael M. Whalen
George Orson
Wheat "Whipsaw"
H. C. Wills
Elijah Nicholas Wilson

Slim Wilson
Joseph Barney Wintle
Henry Worley
James Worthington
George Wright
Mose Wright
Jose Zowgaltz

Timeline

1846 The Donner party is stranded at Donner's Pass.
1847 Mormons under Brigham Young migrate to Utah.
1848 Gold rush fever hits the eastern and midwestern states.
1850 California achieves statehood and proclaims itself a free state.
1854 The Republican Party is formed to combat the growing power of the Southern states.
1858 Chief Winnemucca signs a treaty with white settlers and helps them drive out the Pit tribes who were raiding settler potato fields.
1860 Russell, Majors & Waddell announce they are launching the Pony Express; the first run begins on April 3; Abraham Lincoln is elected president in November; South Carolina secedes in December.
1861 The Civil War begins; telegraph lines from the east and west meet and join at Salt Lake City on October 26; Pony Express riders finish up their last laps and move on to other employment.

Sources

CHAPTER ONE: From the East

p. 13, "GREAT EXPRESS ADVENTURE..." Raymond Settles and Mary Settles, *Saddles and Spurs: The Pony Express Saga* (Lincoln: University of Nebraska Press, 1972), 35.

p. 18, "While I am in the . . ." Ibid., 8.

CHAPTER NINE: Stories and Legends

p. 131, "They respected courage . . ." Rowe Findley, "A Buckaroo Stew of Fact and Legend, The Pony Express," *National Geographic* (July 1980), 64.

CHAPTER TEN: Another Try

p. 145-146, "The union of these . . ." George Brown Tindall and David E. Shi, *America: A Narrative History,* Brief Fifth Edition (New York: W.W. Norton & Company, 2000), 546.

CHAPTER ELEVEN: The End of the Pony Express

p. 161, "You came to us . . ." Findley, "A Buckaroo Stew," 71.

Bibliography

Bancroft, Hubert Howe. *The Works of Hubert Howe Bancroft*. Volume VII, *History of California, 1860-1890*. San Francisco: The History Company Publishers, 1890.

———. *The Works of Hubert Howe Bancroft*. Volume XXV, *History of Nevada, California, and Wyoming, 1640-1888*. San Francisco: The History Company Publishers, 1890.

———. *The Works of Hubert Howe Bancroft*. Volume XXVI, *History of Utah, 1840-1886*. San Francisco: The History Company Publishers, 1890.

Bensen, Joe. *Travelers' Guide to the Pony Express Trail*. Helena, MT: Falcon Press, 1995.

Blake, Herbert Cody. *Blake Western Stories*. Brooklyn, NY: Herbert Cody Blake Publishers, 1829.

Bloss, Roy S. *Pony Express: The Great Gamble*. Berkley, CA: Howell-North Press, 1959.

Boggs, Mae B. *My Playhouse was a Concord Coach*. Oakland, CA: Howell-North Press, 1942.

Bradley, Glenn D. *The Story of the Pony Express*. Chicago: A. C. McClurg & Company, 1913.

Bristow, J. T. *The Overland Mail: Old Military Road and Pony Express Route*. Horton, KS: Charles B. Browne and the Headlight Printshop, 1937.

Burton, Richard F. *The City of the Saints and Across the Rocky Mountains to California.* New York: Harper and Brothers Publishers, 1862.

Cody, Bill. *An Autobiography of Buffalo Bill and Wild Bill Hickock.* New York: Cosmopolitan Book Corporation, 1920.

Conkling, Roscoe P. and Margaret B. *The Butterfield Overland Mail, 1857-1869.* Glendale, California: A. B. Clarke Company, 1947.

Cordes, Kathleen Anne and Jane Lammers. *America's National Historic Trails.* Norman: University of Oklahoma Press, 1999.

Driggs, Howard R. *The Pony Express Goes Through.* New York: Frederick A. Stokes Company, 1935.

Egan, Howard. *Pioneering in the West, 1846-1878 Major Howard Egan's Diary.* Salt Lake City, UT: Skelton Publishing Company, 1917.

Findley, Rowe. "The Pony Express." *National Geographic.* July 1980.

Gorenfeld, William and John. "Punishing the Paiutes." *Wild West.* December 2001.

Howard, Robert West, Roy E. Robertson, Frank C. and Agnes Wright Spring, *Hoofbeats of Destiny.* New York: Clarkson N. Potter, Inc., 1960.

Jensen, Lee. *The Pony Express.* New York: Grosset & Dunlap Publishers, 1955.

Lewis, Oscar. *San Francisco: Mission to Metropolis.* San Diego: Howell, North Books, 1988.

Loomis, Noel M. *Wells Fargo.* New York: Clarkson N. Potter, Inc., 1968.

Nevin, David and the editors of Time-Life Books. *The Old West: The Expressmen.* New York: Time-Life Books, 1974.

Ormsby, Waterman. *The Butterfield Overland Mail.* San Marino, CA: Huntington Library, 1954.

Reinfield, Fred. *Pony Express.* Lincoln: University of Nebraska Press, 1973.

Settle, Raymond W. and Mary L. *Empire on Wheels.* Stanford, CA: Stanford University Press, 1949.

———. *Saddles and Spurs: The Pony Express Saga.* Harrisburg, PA: The Stackpole Company, 1955.

———. *War Drums and Wagon Wheels: The Story of Russell, Majors & Waddell.* Lincoln: University of Nebraska Press, 1983.

Twain, Mark. *Roughing It.* New York: Airmont Publishing Co., 1967.

Web sites

http://www.nps.gov/poex/
A guide to the Pony Express National Historic Trail, maintained by the National Park Service.

http://www.ponyexpress.org/
The online home of the Pony Express National Museum, located in St. Joseph, Missouri, and housed in the same building that once served as the Pike's Peak Stables.

http://www.xphomestation.com/index.html
An extensive Pony Express-related site developed and maintained by amateur historian Tom Crews. A great resource for students and teachers.

http://www.sfmuseum.org/hist1/pxpress.html
The Virtual Museum of the City of San Francisco explores the relationship of the Pony Express to that city's history.

http://www.postalmuseum.si.edu/index.html
The Smithsonian National Postal Museum traces the history of mail delivery in the United States.

http://plpt.nsn.us/
The online home of the Pyramid Lake Paiute tribe's reservation.

Index